| 111TH CONGRESS | COMMITTEE PRINT | S. PRT. |
| 1st Session | | 111○?? |

TORA BORA REVISITED: HOW WE FAILED TO GET BIN LADEN AND WHY IT MATTERS TODAY

A Report To Members

OF THE

COMMITTEE ON FOREIGN RELATIONS UNITED STATES SENATE

John F. Kerry, Chairman

ONE HUNDRED ELEVENTH CONGRESS
FIRST SESSION

NOVEMBER 30, 2009

Printed for the use of the Committee on Foreign Relations

Available via World Wide Web: http://www.gpoaccess.gov/congress/index.html

U.S. GOVERNMENT PRINTING OFFICE

??–??? PDF   WASHINGTON : 2009

For sale by the Superintendent of Documents, U.S. Government Printing Office
Internet: bookstore.gpo.gov   Phone: toll free (866) 512–1800; DC area (202) 512–1800
Fax: (202) 512–2104   Mail: Stop IDCC, Washington, DC 20402–0001

COMMITTEE ON FOREIGN RELATIONS

JOHN F. KERRY, Massachusetts, *Chairman*

CHRISTOPHER J. DODD, Connecticut
RUSSELL D. FEINGOLD, Wisconsin
BARBARA BOXER, California
ROBERT MENENDEZ, New Jersey
BENJAMIN L. CARDIN, Maryland
ROBERT P. CASEY, JR., Pennsylvania
JIM WEBB, Virginia
JEANNE SHAHEEN, New Hampshire
EDWARD E. KAUFMAN, Delaware
KIRSTEN E. GILLIBRAND, New York

RICHARD G. LUGAR, Indiana
BOB CORKER, Tennessee
JOHNNY ISAKSON, Georgia
JAMES E. RISCH, Idaho
JIM DeMINT, South Carolina
JOHN BARRASSO, Wyoming
ROGER F. WICKER, Mississippi
JAMES M. INHOF, Oklahoma

DAVID McKean, *Staff Director*
KENNETH A. MYERS, JR., *Republican Staff Director*

CONTENTS

	Page
Letter of Transmittal	v
Executive Summary	1
1. Flight to Tora Bora	3
The Sheikh Arrives	5
Other Voices, Same Conclusion	7
"A Controversial Fight"	9
2. The Afghan Model: A Flawed Masterpiece or Just Flawed?	10
A Shift in Attention and Resources	12
"We're Going to Lose Our Prey"	13
Flight from Tora Bora	13
3. An Alternative Plan	15
Troops Were Ready to Go	17
The Price of Failure	19
Endnotes	21

APPENDIXES

Appendix I.—"A Flawed Masterpiece," Michael E. O'Hanlon, *Foreign Affairs*, March/April 2002	25
Appendix II.—United States Special Operations Command History, 6th Edition	33

LETTER OF TRANSMITTAL

UNITED STATES SENATE,
COMMITTEE ON FOREIGN RELATIONS,
Washington, DC, November 30, 2009.

DEAR COLLEAGUE: This report by the Committee majority staff is part of our continuing examination of the conflict in Afghanistan. When we went to war less than a month after the attacks of September 11, the objective was to destroy Al Qaeda and kill or capture its leader, Osama bin Laden, and other senior figures in the terrorist group and the Taliban, which had hosted them. Today, more than eight years later, we find ourselves fighting an increasingly lethal insurgency in Afghanistan and neighboring Pakistan that is led by many of those same extremists. Our inability to finish the job in late 2001 has contributed to a conflict today that endangers not just our troops and those of our allies, but the stability of a volatile and vital region. This report relies on new and existing information to explore the consequences of the failure to eliminate bin Laden and other extremist leaders in the hope that we can learn from the mistakes of the past.

Sincerely,

JOHN F. KERRY,
Chairman.

TORA BORA REVISITED: HOW WE FAILED TO GET BIN LADEN AND WHY IT MATTERS TODAY

EXECUTIVE SUMMARY

On October 7, 2001, U.S. aircraft began bombing the training bases and strongholds of Al Qaeda and the ruling Taliban across Afghanistan. The leaders who sent murderers to attack the World Trade Center and the Pentagon less than a month earlier and the rogue government that provided them sanctuary were running for their lives. President George W. Bush's expression of America's desire to get Osama bin Laden "dead or alive" seemed about to come true.

Two months later, American civilian and military leaders celebrated what they viewed as a lasting victory with the selection of Hamid Karzai as the country's new hand-picked leader. The war had been conceived as a swift campaign with a single objective: defeat the Taliban and destroy Al Qaeda by capturing or killing bin Laden and other key leaders. A unique combination of airpower, Central Intelligence Agency and special operations forces teams and indigenous allies had swept the Taliban from power and ousted Al Qaeda from its safe haven while keeping American deaths to a minimum. But even in the initial glow, there were concerns: The mission had failed to capture or kill bin Laden.

Removing the Al Qaeda leader from the battlefield eight years ago would not have eliminated the worldwide extremist threat. But the decisions that opened the door for his escape to Pakistan allowed bin Laden to emerge as a potent symbolic figure who continues to attract a steady flow of money and inspire fanatics worldwide. The failure to finish the job represents a lost opportunity that forever altered the course of the conflict in Afghanistan and the future of international terrorism, leaving the American people more vulnerable to terrorism, laying the foundation for today's protracted Afghan insurgency and inflaming the internal strife now endangering Pakistan. Al Qaeda shifted its locus across the border into Pakistan, where it has trained extremists linked to numerous plots, including the July 2005 transit bombings in London and two recent aborted attacks involving people living in the United States. The terrorist group's resurgence in Pakistan has coincided with the rising violence orchestrated in Afghanistan by the Taliban, whose leaders also escaped only to re-emerge to direct today's increasingly lethal Afghan insurgency.

This failure and its enormous consequences were not inevitable. By early December 2001, Bin Laden's world had shrunk to a complex of caves and tunnels carved into a mountainous section of eastern Afghanistan known as Tora Bora. Cornered in some of the most forbidding terrain on earth, he and several hundred of his men, the largest concentration of Al Qaeda fighters of the war, endured relentless pounding by American aircraft, as many as 100 air strikes a day. One 15,000-pound bomb, so huge it had to be rolled out the back of a C-130 cargo plane, shook the mountains for miles. It seemed only a matter of time before U.S. troops and their Afghan allies overran the remnants of Al Qaeda hunkered down in the thin, cold air at 14,000 feet.

Bin Laden expected to die. His last will and testament, written on December 14, reflected his fatalism. "Allah commended to us that when death approaches any of us that we make a bequest to parents and next of kin and to Muslims as a whole," he wrote, according to a copy of the will that surfaced later and is regarded as authentic. "Allah bears witness that the love of jihad and death in the cause of Allah has dominated my life and the verses of the sword permeated every cell in my heart, 'and fight the pagans all together as they fight you all together.' How many times did I wake up to find myself reciting this holy verse!" He instructed his wives not to remarry and apologized to his children for devoting himself to jihad.

But the Al Qaeda leader would live to fight another day. Fewer than 100 American commandos were on the scene with their Afghan allies and calls for reinforcements to launch an assault were rejected. Requests were also turned down for U.S. troops to block the mountain paths leading to sanctuary a few miles away in Pakistan. The vast array of American military power, from sniper teams to the most mobile divisions of the Marine Corps and the Army, was kept on the sidelines. Instead, the U.S. command chose to rely on airstrikes and untrained Afghan militias to attack bin Laden and on Pakistan's loosely organized Frontier Corps to seal his escape routes. On or around December 16, two days after writing his will, bin Laden and an entourage of bodyguards walked unmolested out of Tora Bora and disappeared into Pakistan's unregulated tribal area. Most analysts say he is still there today.

The decision not to deploy American forces to go after bin Laden or block his escape was made by Secretary of Defense Donald Rumsfeld and his top commander, Gen. Tommy Franks, the architects of the unconventional Afghan battle plan known as Operation Enduring Freedom. Rumsfeld said at the time that he was concerned that too many U.S. troops in Afghanistan would create an anti-American backlash and fuel a widespread insurgency. Reversing the recent American military orthodoxy known as the Powell doctrine, the Afghan model emphasized minimizing the U.S. presence by relying on small, highly mobile teams of special operations troops and CIA paramilitary operatives working with the Afghan opposition. Even when his own commanders and senior intelligence officials in Afghanistan and Washington argued for dispatching more U.S. troops, Franks refused to deviate from the plan.

There were enough U.S. troops in or near Afghanistan to execute the classic sweep-and-block maneuver required to attack bin Laden and try to prevent his escape. It would have been a dangerous fight across treacherous terrain, and the injection of more U.S. troops and the resulting casualties would have contradicted the risk-averse, "light footprint" model formulated by Rumsfeld and Franks. But commanders on the scene and elsewhere in Afghanistan argued that the risks were worth the reward.

After bin Laden's escape, some military and intelligence analysts and the press criticized the Pentagon's failure to mount a full-scale attack despite the tough rhetoric by President Bush. Franks, Vice President Dick Cheney and others defended the decision, arguing that the intelligence was inconclusive about the Al Qaeda leader's location. But the review of existing literature, unclassified government records and interviews with central participants underlying this report removes any lingering doubts and makes it clear that Osama bin Laden was within our grasp at Tora Bora.

For example, the CIA and Delta Force commanders who spent three weeks at Tora Bora as well as other intelligence and military sources are certain he was there. Franks' second-in-command during the war, retired Lt. Gen. Michael DeLong, wrote in his autobiography that bin Laden was "definitely there when we hit the caves"—a statement he retracted when the failure became a political issue. Most authoritatively, the official history of the U.S. Special Operations Command determined that bin Laden was at Tora Bora. "All source reporting corroborated his presence on several days from 9-14 December," said a declassified version of the history, which was based on accounts of commanders and intelligence officials and published without fanfare two years ago.

The reasons behind the failure to capture or kill Osama bin Laden and its lasting consequences are examined over three sections in this report. The first section traces bin Laden's path from southern Afghanistan to the mountains of Tora Bora and lays out new and previous evidence that he was there. The second explores new information behind the decision not to launch an assault. The final section examines the military options that might have led to his capture or death at Tora Bora and the ongoing impact of the failure to bring him back "dead or alive."

1. FLIGHT TO TORA BORA

Whether Osama bin Laden was at Tora Bora in late 2001 has been the topic of heated debate since he escaped Afghanistan to the tribal belt of Pakistan. The evidence is convincing that the Al Qaeda leader was in the mountains of eastern Afghanistan in that critical period. The information comes from U.S. military officers at Tora Bora, from detainees who were in the camps with bin Laden, from the senior CIA officer in Afghanistan at the time, and from the official history of the special operations forces. Based on that evidence, it is clear that the Al Qaeda leader was within reach of U.S. troops three months after the attacks on New York and Washington.

In the middle of August 2001, two Pakistani nuclear scientists sat down in a mud-walled compound on the outskirts of Kandahar in southern Afghanistan, the spiritual and tactical headquarters of Taliban fundamentalists who controlled most of the country. Seated with them were bin Laden and Ayman al-Zawahiri, the Egyptian surgeon who was his chief deputy and strategist. The four men spent two days discussing Al Qaeda's determination to obtain nuclear weapons before bin Laden and Zawahiri abruptly excused themselves and left the compound. Before departing, bin Laden promised the Pakistanis that something momentous was going to happen soon.

American intelligence had already picked up indications that something momentous was coming. George Tenet, who was director of central intelligence at the time, later testified before the 9/11 Commission that the "system was blinking red" from July 2001 until the actual attacks. The first reports of possible attacks on the United States had been picked up in June and the warnings increased steadily from then on. On July 12, Tenet went to Capitol Hill to provide a top-secret briefing for senators about the rising threat of an imminent attack. Only a handful of senators turned up in S-407, the secure conference room in the Capitol, to hear the CIA director warn that he was extremely worried that bin Laden and Al Qaeda were preparing an attack on U.S. soil. Tenet told them the attack was not a question of *if,* but *when.*

Less than a month later, on August 6, President Bush's daily briefing repeated the warning under the ominous headline "Bin Ladin Determined To Strike in US." The text described previous plots carried out by Al Qaeda against American targets overseas and said the FBI had uncovered "patterns of suspicious activity in this country consistent with preparations for hijackings or other types of attacks, including recent surveillance of federal buildings in New York." At the time, President Bush later told the 9/11 Commission that he regarded the warning as historical in nature. The commission's voluminous report said its investigators "found no indication of any further discussion before September 11 among the president and his top advisers of the possibility of a threat of an Al Qaeda attack in the United States."

Bin Laden's movements in the days surrounding September 11 remain sketchy. Some facts have emerged from reputable journalists, U.S. military and intelligence sources and Afghans who said they saw the Al Qaeda leader at various points along his path to Tora Bora. He was spotted in Khost in eastern Afghanistan around September 11. On November 8, he and Zawahiri met in Kabul with Hamid Mir, a respected Pakistani journalist. By then, U.S. special operations forces and Northern Alliance troops were closing in on the Afghan capital. The Al Qaeda leaders had risked the trip to attend a memorial service honoring the Uzbek militant leader Juma Khan Namangani, who had been killed in a U.S. airstrike. Before Kabul fell, bin Laden and Zawahiri traveled five hours east to the ancient trading center of Jalalabad. From there, by all reliable accounts, they went to ground at Tora Bora, one of bin Laden's old haunts from the days of fighting the Soviets in the 1980s.

Tora Bora is a district about 30 miles southeast of Jalalabad. Rather than a single place, the name covers a fortress-like section of the White Mountains that stretches about six miles long and six miles wide across a collection of narrow valleys, snow-covered ridgelines and jagged peaks reaching 14,000 feet. During the 1980s, when he was fighting the Soviets in Afghanistan, bin Laden turned the site into a formidable stronghold. He built a rough road from Jalalabad and brought in heavy equipment to fortify the natural caves and dig new ones. He supervised the excavation of connecting tunnels so fighters could move unseen between locations in the fights against Soviet troops.

After the defeat of the Soviet Union in 1989, bin Laden left Afghanistan and eventually set up the operations of his fledgling terrorist organization in the northeastern African nation of Sudan. After pressure from the United States, Sudan expelled bin Laden in 1996 and he flew with his wives and children to Jalalabad on a chartered jet. Upon his return to Afghanistan, bin Laden began expanding the fortress at Tora Bora, building base camps at higher elevations for himself, his wives and numerous children, and other senior Al Qaeda figures. Some rooms were reported to be concealed 350 feet inside the granite peaks. The mountainsides leading to those upper reaches were steep and pitted with well-built bunkers cloaked in camouflage. In the years that followed, Bin Laden got to know the surrounding geography well from spending hours on long hikes with his children. His familiarity with the worn trails used over the centuries by traders and smugglers to traverse the few miles into Pakistan would serve him well.

The United States rightly anticipated that bin Laden would make his last stand at Tora Bora. The precise dates of his arrival and departure are hard to pin down, but it's clear that U.S. intelligence picked up his trail well before he got there. The CIA had evidence that bin Laden was headed for the mountain redoubt by early November, according to Tenet, the former CIA director. Outside experts like Peter Bergen, the last American to interview bin Laden, estimate that he arrived by the end of November, along with 1,000 to 1,500 hardened fighters and bodyguards. In a television interview on November 29, 2001, Vice President Cheney said he believed the Al Qaeda leader was in the general area of Tora Bora. "He's got a large number of fighters with him probably, a fairly secure personal security force that he has some degree of confidence in, and he'll have to try to leave, that is, he may depart for other territory, but that's not quite as easy as it would have been a few months ago," Cheney said.

The Sheikh Arrives

Bin Laden's presence was more than conjecture. A major with the Army's Delta Force, who is now retired and uses the pen name Dalton Fury, was the senior U.S. military officer at Tora Bora, commanding about 90 special operations troops and support personnel. He and his fellow commandos from the elite and secretive Delta Force arrived in early December, setting up headquarters in a former schoolhouse near the mountains alongside a handful of CIA operatives who were already there. The Americans were there to direct airstrikes on Tora Bora and work with Afghan militias assembled by two local warlords who had been paid by the CIA to help flush out bin Laden and the Al Qaeda contingent. The Delta Force soldiers were disguised to blend in with the Afghan militia, wearing local clothing, growing bushy beards and sometimes carrying the same types of weapons.

Fury recounted his experiences in a book, Kill Bin Laden, which was published in 2008. He expanded on them in interviews with Committee staff. Both the book and the interviews left no doubt that Fury's team knew bin Laden was holed up at Tora Bora and that he was eager to go get him. In the interviews, he explained that Al Qaeda fighters arrayed in the mountains used unsecure radios, which meant their communications were easily intercepted by his team and by a sophisticated listening post a few miles from the mountain. As a result, the Delta Force and CIA operatives had real-time eavesdropping capabilities on Al Qaeda almost from their arrival, allowing them to track movements and gauge the effectiveness of the bombing. Even more valuable, a few days after arriving, one of the CIA operatives picked up a radio from a dead Al Qaeda fighter. The radio gave the Americans a clear channel into the group's communications on the mountain. Bin Laden's voice was often picked up, along with frequent comments about the presence of the man referred to by his followers as "the sheikh."

Fury, who still uses his pen name to protect his identity, said there was no doubt the voice on the radios was bin Laden. "The CIA had a guy with them called Jalal and he was the foremost expert on bin Laden's voice," he said. "He worked on bin Laden's voice for seven years and he knew him better than anyone else in the West. To him, it was very clear that bin Laden was there on the mountain."

Another special operations expert who speaks fluent Arabic and heard the intercepted communications in real time in Afghanistan told the Committee staff that it was clearly bin Laden's voice. He had studied the Al Qaeda leader's speech pattern and word choices before the war and he said he considered the communications a perfect match.

Afghan villagers who were providing food and other supplies for the Al Qaeda fighters at Tora Bora also confirmed bin Laden's presence. Fury said some of the villagers were paid by the CIA for information about precise locations of clusters of fighters that could be targeted for bombing runs. The locals also provided fragmentary information on bin Laden's movements within the Al Qaeda compound, though the outsiders never got near the sheikh. The cooperating villagers were given rudimentary global positioning devices and told to push a button at any spot where they saw significant numbers of fighters or arms caches. When the locals turned in the devices to collect their payments, the GPS coordinates recorded by pushing the buttons were immediately passed along to targeting officers, who programmed the coordinates into bombing runs.

For several days in early December, Fury's special ops troops moved up the mountains in pairs with fighters from the Afghan militias. The Americans used GPS devices and laser range finders to pinpoint caves and pockets of enemy fighters for the bombers. The Delta Force units were unable to hold any high ground because the Afghans insisted on retreating to their base at the bottom of the mountains each night, leaving the Americans alone inside Al Qaeda territory. Still, it was clear from what they could see and what they were hearing in the intercepted conversations that relentless bombing was taking its toll.

On December 9, a C-130 cargo plane dropped a 15,000-pound bomb, known as a Daisy Cutter, on the Tora Bora complex. The weapon had not been used since Vietnam and there were early fears that its impact had not been as great as expected. But later reports confirmed that the bomb struck with massive force. A captured Al Qaeda fighter who was there later told American interrogators that men deep in caves had been vaporized in what he called "a hideous explosion." That day and others, Fury described intercepting radio communications in which Al Qaeda fighters called for the "red truck to move wounded" and frantic pleas from a fighter to his commander, saying "cave too hot, can't reach others."

At one point, the Americans listened on the radio as bin Laden exhorted his men to keep fighting, though he apologized "for getting them trapped . and pounded by American airstrikes." On December 11, Fury said bin Laden was heard on the radio telling his men that he had let them down and it was okay to surrender. Fury hoped the battle was over, but he would soon determine that it was part of an elaborate ruse to allow Al Qaeda fighters to slip out of Tora Bora for Pakistan.

Fury is adamant that bin Laden was at Tora Bora until mid-December. "There is no doubt that bin Laden was in Tora Bora during the fighting," he wrote in Kill Bin Laden. "From alleged sightings to the radio intercepts to news reports from various countries, it was repeatedly confirmed that he was there."

Other Voices, Same Conclusion

Fury was not alone in his conviction. In some cases, confirmation that bin Laden was at Tora Bora has come from detainees at Guantanamo Bay. A "summary of evidence" prepared by the Pentagon for the trial of an unnamed detainee says flatly that the man "assisted in the escape of Osama bin Laden from Tora Bora." The detainee was described as one of bin Laden's commanders in the fight against the Soviets. The document, which was released to the Associated Press in 2005 through a Freedom of Information request, was the first definitive statement by the Pentagon that the mastermind of 9/11 was at Tora Bora during the American bombing before slipping away into Pakistan.

Another confirmation came from the senior CIA paramilitary commander in Afghanistan at the time. Gary Berntsen was working at the CIA's counterterrorist center in October 2001 when his boss summoned him to the front office and told him, "Gary, I want you killing the enemy immediately." Berntsen left the next day for Afghanistan, where he assumed leadership of the CIA's paramilitary operation against the Taliban and Al Qaeda. His primary target was bin Laden and he was confident that the Al Qaeda leader would make his last stand at Tora Bora. His suspicions were confirmed when he learned bin Laden's voice had been intercepted there.

From the outset, Berntsen says he was skeptical about relying on Afghan militias "cobbled together at the last minute" to capture or kill the man who ordered the 9/11 attacks. "I'd made it clear in my reports that our Afghan allies were hardly anxious to get at al Qaeda in Tora Bora," he wrote in his own book, Jawbreaker, which was published in late 2005. He also knew that the special operations troops and CIA operatives on the scene were not enough to stop bin Laden from escaping across the mountain passes. In the book, Berntsen uses exclamation points to vent his fears that the most wanted man in the world was about to slip out of our grasp.

"We needed U.S. soldiers on the ground!" he wrote. "I'd sent my request for 800 U.S. Army Rangers and was still waiting for a response. I repeated to anyone at headquarters who would listen: We need Rangers now! The opportunity to get bin Laden and his men is slipping away!!"

At one point, Berntsen recalled an argument at a CIA guesthouse in Kabul with Maj. Gen. Dell Dailey, the commander of U.S. special operations forces in Afghanistan at the time. Berntsen said he renewed his demand that American troops be dispatched to Tora Bora immediately. Following orders from Franks at U.S. Central Command (CentCom) headquarters at MacDill Air Force Base in Tampa, Florida, Dailey refused to deploy U.S. troops, explaining that he feared alienating Afghan allies.

"I don't give a damn about offending our allies!" Berntsen shouted. "I only care about eliminating al Qaeda and delivering bin Laden's head in a box!"

Dailey said the military's position was firm and Berntsen replied, "Screw that!"

For those like Franks, who later maintained that bin Laden might not have been at Tora Bora, Berntsen is respectfully scornful. "We could have ended it all there," he said in an interview.

Berntsen's views were generally shared by Gary Schroen, another senior CIA operative in Afghanistan. Schroen, who had spent years cultivating ties to Afghanistan's opposition elements, bemoaned the reliance on local tribal leaders to go after bin Laden and guard escape routes. "Unfortunately, many of those people proved to be loyal to bin Laden and sympathizers with the Taliban and they allowed the key guys to escape," Schroen, who retired from the CIA, said in a television interview in May 2005. He added that he had no doubt that bin Laden was at Tora Bora.

Franks' second-in-command during the war, General DeLong, was convinced that bin Laden was at Tora Bora. In his memoir, Inside CentCom, DeLong described the massive, three-week bombing campaign aimed at killing Al Qaeda fighters in their caves at Tora Bora. "We were hot on Osama bin Laden's trail," he wrote. "He was definitely there when we hit the caves. Every day during the bombing, Rumsfeld asked me, 'Did we get him? Did we get him?' I would have to answer that we didn't know." The retired general said that intelligence suggested bin Laden had been wounded during the bombings before he escaped to Pakistan, a conclusion reached by numerous journalists, too.

DeLong argued that large numbers of U.S. troops could not be dispatched because the area surrounding Tora Bora was controlled by tribes hostile to the United States and other outsiders. But he recognized that the Pakistani Frontier Corps, asked to block any escape attempt by bin Laden, was ill-equipped for the job. "To make matters worse, this tribal area was sympathetic to bin Laden," he wrote. "He was the richest man in the area, and he had funded these people for years."

The book was published in September 2004, a year after DeLong retired from the Army. That fall, the failure to capture or kill bin Laden had become an issue in the presidential campaign. Franks had retired from the Army in 2003 and he often defended the events at Tora Bora. On October 19, 2004, he wrote an opinion article in The New York Times saying that intelligence on the Al Qaeda leader's location had been inconclusive. "We don't know to this day whether Mr. bin Laden was at Tora Bora in December 2001," he wrote. "Some intelligence sources said he was; others indicated he was in Pakistan at the time; still others suggested he was in Kashmir. Tora Bora was teeming with Taliban and Qaeda operatives, many of whom were killed or captured, but Mr. bin Laden was never within our grasp."

Two weeks after the Franks article was published and barely two months after publication of his own book, DeLong reversed the conclusion from his autobiography and echoed his former boss in an opinion article on November 1 in The Wall Street Journal. After defending the decision to rely heavily on local militia and the Pakistani Frontier Corps, DeLong wrote: "Finally, most people fail to realize that it is quite possible that bin Laden was never in Tora Bora to begin with. There exists no concrete intel to prove that he was there at the time."

DeLong said in an interview with Committee staff that the contradiction between his book and the opinion article was the result of murky intelligence. "What I put in the book was what the intel said at the time," he said. "The intel is not always right. I read it that he was there. We even heard that he was injured. Later intel was that he may or may not have been there. Did anybody have eyeballs on him? No. The intel stated that he was there at the time, but we got shot in the face by bad intel many times."

DeLong amplified the reasons for not sending American troops after bin Laden. "The real reason we didn't go in with U.S. troops was that we hadn't had the election yet," he said in the staff interview, a reference to the installation of Hamid Karzai as the interim leader of Afghanistan. "We didn't want to have U.S. forces fighting before Karzai was in power. We wanted to create a stable country and that was more important than going after bin Laden at the time."

"A Controversial Fight"

Military and intelligence officers at Tora Bora have provided ample evidence that bin Laden was there. Al Qaeda detainees have maintained that he was there. And the Pentagon's own summary of evidence in the case against a former senior jihadi commander at Guantanamo Bay concluded the detainee helped bin Laden escape. But the most authoritative and definitive unclassified government document on bin Laden's location in December 2001 is the official history of the United States Special Operations Command.

The Special Operations Command, based alongside CentCom at MacDill Air Force Base, oversees the special forces of the Army, Air Force, Navy and Marine Corps. The heavy reliance on special operations forces during the first stages of the Afghan campaign meant that the command played a central role in executing the war plan. Its units included the Delta Force team on the scene at Tora Bora. In preparing the official history of the command, a team of historians working for the command interviewed military and intelligence officials from every branch of the armed forces. The unclassified version of the history was published in 2007 and includes a lengthy section on the operations at Tora Bora.

The section opens by saying that bin Laden and a large contingent of Al Qaeda troops had fled the area around Kabul for Nangahar Province and its provincial capital, Jalalabad, in early November. "Analysts within both the CIA and CentCom correctly speculated that UBL would make a stand along the northern peaks of the Spin Ghar Mountains at a place then called Tora Gora," says the history. "Tora Bora, as it was redubbed in December, had been a major stronghold of AQ for years and provided routes into Pakistan." The history said bin Laden had "undoubtedly" chosen to make his last stand there prior to the onset of winter, along with between 500 and 2,000 others, before escaping into Pakistan.

In the concluding passage assessing the battle of Tora Bora, the historians from the Special Operations Command wrote: "What has since been determined with reasonable certainty was that UBL was indeed at Tora Bora in December 2001. All source reporting corroborated his presence on several days from 9-14 December. The fact that SOF (special operations forces) came as close to capture or killing UBL as U.S. forces have to date makes Tora Bora a controversial fight. Given the commitment of fewer than 100 American personnel, U.S. forces provide unable to block egress routes from Tora Bora south into Pakistan, the route that UBL most likely took."

Franks declined to respond to any questions about the discrepancies about bin Laden's location or the conclusion of the Special Operations Command historians. "We really don't have time for this," one of his aides, retired Col. Michael T. Hayes, wrote in an email to the Committee staff. "Focused on the future, not the past. Gen Franks made his decisions, based on the intel at the time."

2. THE AFGHAN MODEL: A FLAWED MASTERPIECE OR JUST FLAWED?

Writing in Foreign Affairs in the spring of 2002, the military analyst Michael O'Hanlon declared Operation Enduring Freedom "a masterpiece of military creativity and finesse." The operation had been designed on the fly and O'Hanlon praised Rumsfeld, Franks and CIA Director George Tenet for devising a war plan that combined limited American power and the Afghan opposition to defeat the Taliban and Al Qaeda with only 30 U.S. casualties in the first five months. But O'Hanlon tempered his praise, calling the plan "a flawed masterpiece" because of the failure to capture or kill bin Laden and other enemy leaders. The resurgence of the Taliban and Al Qaeda in recent years, and the turmoil they have wrought in Afghanistan and Pakistan, raise the question of whether the plan was a flawed masterpiece—or simply flawed.

The Afghan model required elite teams of American commandos and CIA paramilitary operatives to form alliances with Afghans who opposed the Taliban and had the militias to help topple the religious fundamentalists. Some of these Afghans were legitimate ethnic and tribal leaders who chafed at the restrictions of the

Taliban and the sanctuary it provided to Al Qaeda. Others were allies of convenience, Taliban rivals who held power by force and paid their men by collecting tolls and taxes on legitimate commerce and trafficking in heroin. By providing money and weapons, the U.S. forces helped the warlords destroy their rivals and expand their personal power. Many later entered the Afghan government and remain influential figures. The strategy was a short cut to victory that would have consequences for long-term stability in Afghanistan.

When it came to bin Laden, the special operations forces relied on two relatively minor warlords from the Jalalabad area. Haji Hazarat Ali had a fourth-grade education and a reputation as a bully. He had fought the Soviets as a teenager in the 1980s and later joined the Taliban for a time. The other, Haji Zaman Ghamsharik, was a wealthy drug smuggler who had been persuaded by the United States to return from France. Ghamsharik also had fought the Soviets, but when the Taliban came to power, he had gone into exile in France. Together, they fielded a force of about 2,000 men, but there were questions from the outset about the competence and loyalties of the fighters. The two warlords and their men distrusted each other and both groups appeared to distrust their American allies.

The Delta Force commandos had doubts about the willingness and ability of the Afghan militias to wage a genuine assault on Tora Bora almost from the outset. Those concerns were underscored each time the Afghans insisted on retreating from the mountains as darkness fell. But the suspicions were confirmed by events that started on the afternoon of December 11.

Haji Ghamsharik approached Fury and told him that Al Qaeda fighters wanted to surrender. He said all they needed to end the siege was a 12-hour ceasefire to allow the fighters to climb down the mountains and turn in their weapons. Intercepted radio chatter seemed to confirm that the fighters had lost their resolve under the relentless bombing and wanted to give up, but Fury remained suspicious.

"This is the greatest day in the history of Afghanistan," Ghamsharik told Fury.

"Why is that?" asked the dubious American officer.

"Because al Qaeda is no more," he said. "Bin Laden is finished."

The Special Operations Command history records that CentCom refused to back the ceasefire, suspecting a ruse, but it said the special ops forces agreed reluctantly to an overnight pause in the bombing to avoid killing the surrendering Al Qaeda fighters. Ghamsharik negotiated by radio with representatives of Al Qaeda. He initially told Fury that a large number of Algerians wanted to surrender. Then he said that he could turn over the entire Al Qaeda leadership. Fury's suspicions increased at such a bold promise. By the morning of December 12, no Al Qaeda fighters had appeared and the Delta Force commander concluded that the whole episode was a hoax. Intelligence estimates are that as many as 800 Al Qaeda fighters escaped that night, but bin Laden stuck it out.

Despite the unreliability of his Afghan allies, Fury refused to give up. He plotted ways to use his 40 Delta Force soldiers and the handful of other special ops troops under his command to go after bin Laden on their own. One of the plans was to go at bin Laden from the one direction he would never anticipate, the southern side of the mountains. "We want to come in on the back door," Fury explained later, pointing on a map to the side of the Tora Bora enclave facing Pakistan. The peaks there rose to 14,000 feet and the valleys and precipitous mountain passes were already deep in snow. "The original plan that we sent up through our higher headquarters, Delta Force wants to come in over the mountain with oxygen, coming from the Pakistan side, over the mountains and come in and get a drop on bin Laden from behind." The audacious assault was nixed somewhere up the chain of command. Undeterred, Fury suggested dropping hundreds of landmines along the passes leading to Pakistan to block bin Laden's escape. "First guy blows his leg off, everybody else stops," he said. "That allows aircraft overhead to find them. They see all these heat sources out there. Okay, there is a big large group of Al Qaeda moving south. They can engage that." That proposal was rejected, too.

About the time Fury was desperately concocting scenarios for going after bin Laden and getting rejections from up the chain of command, Franks was well into planning for the next war—the invasion of Iraq.

A Shift in Attention and Resources

On November 21, 2001, President Bush put his arm on Defense Secretary Rumsfeld as they were leaving a National Security Council meeting at the White House. "I need to see you," the president said. It was 72 days after the 9/11 attacks and just a week after the fall of Kabul. But Bush already had new plans.

According to Bob Woodward's book, *Plan of Attack,* the president said to Rumsfeld: "What kind of a war plan do you have for Iraq? How do you feel about the war plan for Iraq?" Then the president told Woodward he recalled saying: "Let's get started on this. And get Tommy Franks looking at what it would take to protect America by removing Saddam Hussein if we have to." Back at the Pentagon, Rumsfeld convened a meeting of the Joint Chiefs of Staff to draft a message for Franks asking for a new assessment of a war with Iraq. The existing operations plan had been created in 1998 and it hinged on assembling the kind of massive international coalition used in Desert Storm in 1991.

In his memoir, *American General,* Franks later described getting the November 21 telephone call from Rumsfeld relaying the president's orders while he was sitting in his office at MacDill Air Force Base in Florida. Franks and one of his aides were working on air support for the Afghan units being assembled to push into the mountains surrounding Tora Bora. Rumsfeld said the president wanted options for war with Iraq. Franks said the existing plan was out of date and that a new one should include lessons about precision weapons and the use of special operations forces learned in Afghanistan.

"Okay, Tom," Rumsfeld said, according to Franks. "Please dust it off and get back to me next week."

Franks described his reaction to Rumsfeld's orders this way: "Son of a bitch. No rest for the weary."

For critics of the Bush administration's commitment to Afghanistan, the shift in focus just as Franks and his senior aides were literally working on plans for the attacks on Tora Bora represents a dramatic turning point that allowed a sustained victory in Afghanistan to slip through our fingers. Almost immediately, intelligence and military planning resources were transferred to begin planning on the next war in Iraq. Though Fury, Berntsen and others in the field did not know what was happening back at CentCom, the drain in resources and shift in attention would affect them and the future course of the U.S. campaign in Afghanistan.

"We're Going to Lose Our Prey"

In his memoir, *At the Center of the Storm,* former CIA Director Tenet said it was evident from the start that aerial bombing would not be enough to get bin Laden at Tora Bora. Troops needed to be in the caves themselves, he wrote, but the Afghan militiamen were "distinctly reluctant" to put themselves in harm's way and there were not enough Americans on the scene. He said that senior CIA officials lobbied hard for inserting U.S. troops. Henry Crumpton, the head of special operations for the CIA's counterterrorism operation and chief of its Afghan strategy, made direct requests to Franks. Crumpton had told him that the back door to Pakistan was open and urged Franks to move more than 1,000 Marines who had set up a base near Kandahar to Tora Bora to block escape routes. But the CentCom commander rejected the idea, saying it would take weeks to get a large enough U.S. contingent on the scene and bin Laden might disappear in the meantime.

At the end of November, Crumpton went to the White House to brief President Bush and Vice President Cheney and repeated the message that he had delivered to Franks. Crumpton warned the president that the Afghan campaign's primary goal of capturing bin Laden was in jeopardy because of the military's reliance on Afghan militias at Tora Bora. Crumpton showed the president where Tora Bora was located in the White Mountains and described the caves and tunnels that riddled the region. Crumpton questioned whether the Pakistani forces would be able to seal off the escape routes and pointed out that the promised Pakistani troops had not arrived yet. In addition, the CIA officer told the president that the Afghan forces at Tora Bora were "tired and cold" and "they're just not invested in getting bin Laden."

According to author Ron Suskind in *The One Percent Solution,* Crumpton sensed that his earlier warnings to Franks and others at the Pentagon had not been relayed the president. So Crumpton went further, telling Bush that "we're going to lose our prey if we're not careful." He recommended that the Marines or other U.S. troops be rushed to Tora Bora.

"How bad off are these Afghani forces, really?" asked Bush. "Are they up to the job?

"Definitely not, Mr. President," Crumpton replied. "Definitely not."

Flight from Tora Bora

On December 14, the day bin Laden finished his will, Dalton Fury finally convinced Ali and his men to stay overnight in one of the canyons that they had captured during daylight. Over the next three days, the Afghan militia and their American advisers moved steadily through the canyons, calling in airstrikes and taking out lingering pockets of fighters. The resistance seemed to have vanished, prompting Ali to declare victory on December 17. Most of the Tora Bora complex was abandoned and many of the caves and tunnels were buried in debris. Only about 20 stragglers were taken prisoner. The consensus was that Al Qaeda fighters who had survived the fierce bombing had escaped into Pakistan or melted into the local population. Bin Laden was nowhere to be found. Two days later, Fury and his Delta Force colleagues left Tora Bora, hoping that someone would eventually find bin Laden buried in one of the caves.

There was no body because bin Laden did not die at Tora Bora. Later U.S. intelligence reports and accounts by journalists and others said that he and a contingent of bodyguards departed Tora Bora on December 16. With help from Afghans and Pakistanis who had been paid in advance, the group made its way on foot and horseback across the mountain passes and into Pakistan without encountering any resistance.

The Special Operations Command history noted that there were not enough U.S. troops to prevent the escape, acknowledging that the failure to capture or killing bin Laden made Tora Bora a controversial battle. But Franks argued that Tora was a success and he praised both the Afghan militias and the Pakistanis who were supposed to have protected the border. "I think it was a good operation," he said in an interview for the PBS show Frontline on the first anniversary of the Afghan war. "Many people have said, 'Well, gosh, you know bin Laden got away.' I have yet to see anything that proves bin Laden or whomever was there. That's not to say they weren't, but I've not seen proof that they were there."

Bin Laden himself later acknowledged that he was at Tora Bora, boasting about how he and Zawahiri survived the heavy bombing along with 300 fighters before escaping. "The bombardment was round-the-clock and the warplanes continued to fly over us day and night," he said in an audio tape released on February 11, 2003. "Planes poured their lava on us, particularly after accomplishing their main missions in Afghanistan."

In the aftermath of bin Laden's escape, there were accusations that militiamen working for the two warlords hired by the CIA to get him had helped the Al Qaeda leader cross into Pakistan. Michael Scheuer, who spent 15 years working on Afghanistan at the CIA and at one point headed the agency's bin Laden task force, was sharply critical of the war plan from the start because of its reliance on Afghan allies of dubious loyalty. "Everyone who was cognizant of how Afghan operations worked would have told Mr. Tenet that he was nuts," Scheuer said later. "And as it turned out, he was. ... The people we bought, the people Mr. Tenet said we would own, let Osama bin Laden escape from Tora Bora in eastern Afghanistan into Pakistan."

The American forces never had a clear idea how many Al Qaeda fighters were arrayed against them. Estimates ranged as high as 3,000 and as low as 500, but the consensus put the figure around 1,000—at least until so many escaped during the fake surrender.

Regardless of the exact number of enemy fighters, assaulting Tora Bora would have been difficult and probably would have cost many American and Afghan lives. The Special Operations Command's history offered this tightly worded assessment: "With large numbers of well-supplied, fanatical AQ troops dug into extensive fortified positions, Tora Bora appeared to be an extremely tough target."

For Dalton Fury, the reward would have been worth the risk. "In general, I definitely think it was worth the risk to the force to assault Tora Bora for Osama bin Laden," he told the Committee staff. "What other target out there, then or now, could be more important to our nation's struggle in the global war on terror?"

3. AN ALTERNATIVE BATTLE PLAN

Rather than allowing bin Laden to escape, Franks and Rumsfeld could have deployed American troops already in Afghanistan on or near the border with Pakistan to block the exits while simultaneously sending special operations forces and their Afghan allies up the mountains to Tora Bora. The complex mission would have been risky, but analysis shows that it was well within the reach and capability of the American military.

In the years following the Vietnam War, the U.S. military developed a doctrine intended to place new constraints on when the country went to war and to avoid a repeat of the disastrous and prolonged conflict in Southeast Asia. In its most simplistic form, the doctrine focused on applying overwhelming and disproportionate military force to achieve concrete political goals. It called for mobilizing the military and political resources necessary for ending conflicts quickly and leaving no loose ends. The concept was known informally as the Powell doctrine, named for General Colin Powell, who outlined his vision at the end of the Persian Gulf War in 1991.

The Afghan model constructed by Rumsfeld and Franks in response to the attacks on September 11 stood the Powell doctrine on its head. The new template was designed to deliver a swift and economical knockout blow through airpower and the limited application of troops on the ground. Instead of overwhelming force, the Afghan model depended on airpower and on highly mobile special operations forces and CIA paramilitary teams, working in concert with opposition warlords and tribal leaders. It was designed as unconventional warfare led by indigenous forces, and Franks put a ceiling of 10,000 on the number of U.S. troops in Afghanistan. Despite the valor of the limited American forces, the doctrine failed to achieve one of its most concrete political goals—eliminating the leadership of Al Qaeda and the Taliban. The result has turned out to be nothing close to decisive victory followed by quick withdrawal.

Assembling the size force required to apply overwhelming force across a country as large and rugged as Afghanistan would have taken many weeks. The only country in the region likely to provide the major bases required to prepare an invasion by tens of thousands of troops was Pakistan, and political sensitivities there would have made full cooperation both doubtful and risky for its leadership. The Pakistanis provided limited bases for U.S. operations in the early stages of planning and the invasion; the footprint was kept small to avoid a public outcry. But soldiers and scholars alike have argued that there were sufficient troops available in Afghanistan and nearby Uzbekistan to mount a genuine assault on Osama bin Laden's position at Tora Bora. And they could have been augmented within about a week by reinforcements from the Persian Gulf and the United States.

The most detailed description of the assault option was laid out in an article in the journal *Security Studies* by Peter John Paul Krause of Massachusetts Institute of Technology. Entitled "The Last Good Chance: A Reassessment of U.S. Operations at Tora Bora," the article described a large-scale operation called a block and sweep. The plan is simple enough: One group of American forces would block the likely exit avenues to Pakistan on the south side of Tora Bora while a second contingent moved against Al Qaeda's positions from the north. Simplicity should not be mistaken for sure success: Variables like weather conditions, the effectiveness of the remaining Al Qaeda fighters and the ability to close the escape routes would have made the mission risky. The dangers of attacking fortified positions manned by hardened fighters would likely have resulted in significant U.S. casualties.

The assault would not have required thousands of conventional forces. A large number of troops would have taken too long to deploy and alerted Al Qaeda to the approaching attack. "My opinion is that bin Laden would have left even earlier as soon as he received word that the U.S. troops were surrounding him," Fury told the Committee staff. "I think he only stayed as long as he did because he thought the mujahedin would not aggressively pursue him."

The preferred choice would have been a small, agile force capable of deploying quickly and quietly and trained to operate in difficult terrain against unconventional enemies. The U.S. military has large numbers of soldiers and Marines who meet those criteria—Delta Force, Green Berets, Navy Seals, Marine special operations units and Army Rangers and paratroopers. The effectiveness of U.S. special operations commandos, even in small numbers, was demonstrated on December 10. Two U.S. soldiers were able to get close enough to the Al Qaeda positions to call in air strikes for 17 straight hours, forcing enemy fighters to retreat and enabling the Afghan militia to capture key terrain near bin Laden's suspected location. It was an example of what a larger U.S. force could have accomplished, with support from available air power.

The CIA's Berntsen had requested a battalion of Rangers, about 800 soldiers, and been turned down by CentCom. A battalion would have been a substantial increase in the U.S. presence, but it probably would not have been enough to both assault the stronghold from the north and block the exits on the south. Krause estimated that as few as 500 troops could have carried out the initial northern assault, with reinforcements arriving over the course of the battle. At least twice as many troops would have been required to execute the blocking mission on the southern, eastern and western reaches of Tora Bora. Krause proposed spreading about 1,500 troops to capture or kill anyone trying to flee. O'Hanlon estimated that closing off escape routes to Pakistan would have required 1,000 to 3,000 American troops. In all, an initial force of roughly 2,000 to 3,000 troops would have been sufficient to begin the block-and-sweep mission, with reinforcements following as time and circumstances allowed.

Troops Were Ready to Go

Assembling the troops to augment the handful of special ops commandos under Fury's leadership at Tora Bora would have been a manageable task. Franks had set the ceiling of 10,000 U.S. troops to maintain a light footprint. Still, within that number there were enough ready and willing to go after bin Laden. In late November, about the time U.S. intelligence placed bin Laden squarely at Tora Bora, more than 1,000 members of the 15th and 26th Marine Expeditionary Units, among the military's most mobile arms, established a base southwest of Kandahar, only a few hours flight away. They were primarily interdicting traffic and supporting the special operations teams working with Afghan militias. Another 1,000 troops from the Army's 10th Mountain Division were split between a base in southern Uzbekistan and Bagram Air Base, a short helicopter flight from Tora Bora. The Army troops were engaged mainly in military police functions, according to reports at the time.

Both forces are trained in unconventional warfare and could have been redeployed rapidly for an assault. Lt. Col. Paul Lacamera, commander of a 10th Mountain battalion, later said that his men had been prepared to deploy anywhere in Afghanistan since mid-November. "We weren't just sitting there digging holes and looking out," said Lacamera, whose actions in a later assault on Al Qaeda forces won him a Silver Star. "We were training for potential fights because eventually it was going to come to that."

The commander of the Marines outside Kandahar, Brig. Gen. James N. Mattis, told a journalist that his troops could seal off Tora Bora, but his superiors rejected the plan. Everyone knew that such an operation would have conflicted with the Afghan model laid down by Franks and Rumsfeld. But there were other reasons to hesitate. One former officer told the Committee staff that the inability to get sufficient medical-evacuation helicopters into the rough terrain was a major stumbling block for those who considered trying to push for the assault. He also said there were worries that bad weather would ground transport helicopters or, worse, knock them out of the sky.

In addition to the troops in country, a battalion of Army Rangers was stationed in the Persian Gulf country of Oman, and 200 of them had demonstrated their abilities by parachuting into an airfield near Kandahar at night in October. In Krause's analysis, a battalion of about 800 soldiers from the 82nd Airborne Division at Fort Bragg, North Carolina, could have been deployed to Tora Bora in less than a week, covering the 7,000 miles in C-17 transport aircraft.

No one should underestimate the logistical difficulty and danger of deploying even specially trained troops into hostile territory at altitudes of 7,000 to 10,000 feet. Landing zones for helicopters would likely have come under fire from Al Qaeda positions and drop zones for paratroopers were few and far between in the jagged terrain. But Chinook helicopters, the work horse for rapid deployments, proved capable of carrying combat troops above 11,000-foot mountain ranges as part of Operation Anaconda, a similar block-and-sweep mission carried out in February 2002 in eastern Afghanistan.

Former U.S. military officers said that sending American troops into Tora Bora was discussed at various times in late November and early December of 2001. The CIA's Afghan chief, Hank Crumpton, made specific requests to Franks for U.S. troops and urged President Bush not to rely on Afghan militias and Pakistani paramilitary troops to do the job. CentCom went so far as to develop a plan to put several thousand U.S. troops into Tora Bora. Commanders estimated that deploying 1,000 to 3,000 American troops would have required several hundred airlift flights by helicopters over a week or more.

DeLong defended the decision not to deploy large numbers of American troops. "We didn't have the lift," he told the Committee staff. "We didn't have the medical capabilities. The further we went down the road, the easier the decision got. We wanted Afghanistan to be peaceful for Karzai to take over. Right or not, that was the thinking behind what we did."

The Afghan model proved effective in some instances, particularly when Afghan opposition forces working with American advisers were arrayed against poorly trained Taliban foot soldiers. The precision bombs and overwhelming airpower also played a major role in dispersing the Taliban forces and opening the way for the rapid takeover of the country, though critics now say scattering the Taliban simply allowed them to regroup later. In the early days at Tora Bora, the light footprint allowed a handful of CIA and special operations operatives to guide bombs that killed dozens, if not hundreds, of Al Qaeda fighters. But the model was ineffective when it came to motivating opposition militiamen of questionable skills and doubtful resolve to carry the fight to the biggest concentration of Al Qaeda fighters of the war, particularly when the jihadis were battling to protect their leader. Fewer than 100 special operations force soldiers and CIA operatives were unable to turn the tide against those odds.

Some critics said bin Laden escaped because the United States relied too heavily on Afghan militias to carry the fight forward at Tora Bora and on Pakistan's paramilitary Frontier Corps to block any escape. As Michael O'Hanlon pointed out, our allies did not have the same incentives to stop bin Laden and his associates as American troops. Nor did they have the technology and training to carry out such a difficult mission. The responsibility for allowing the most wanted man in the world to virtually disappear into thin air lies with the American commanders who refused to commit the necessary U.S. soldiers and Marines to finish the job.

The same shortage of U.S. troops allowed Mullah Mohammed Omar and other Taliban leaders to escape. A semi-literate leader who fled Kandahar on a motorbike, Mullah Omar has re-emerged at the helm of the Taliban-led insurgency, which has grown more sophisticated and lethal in recent years and now controls swaths of Afghanistan. The Taliban, which is aligned with a loose network of other militant groups and maintains ties to Al Qaeda, has established shadow governments in many of Afghanistan's provinces and is capable of mounting increasingly complex attacks on American and NATO forces. Bruce Riedel, a former CIA officer who helped develop the Obama administration's Afghan policy, recently referred to the mullah's return to power "one of the most remarkable military comebacks in modern history."

Ironically, one of the guiding principles of the Afghan model was to avoid immersing the United States in a protracted insurgency by sending in too many troops and stirring up anti-American sentiment. In the end, the unwillingness to bend the operational plan to deploy the troops required to take advantage of solid intelligence and unique circumstances to kill or capture bin Laden paved the way for exactly what we had hoped to avoid—a protracted insurgency that has cost more lives than anyone estimates would have been lost in a full-blown assault on Tora Bora. Further, the dangerous contagion of rising violence and instability in Afghanistan has spread to Pakistan, a nuclear-armed ally of the United States which is now wracked by deadly terrorist bombings as it conducts its own costly military campaign against a domestic, Taliban-related insurgency.

The Price of Failure

Osama bin Laden's demise would not have erased the worldwide threat from extremists. But the failure to kill or capture him has allowed bin Laden to exert a malign influence over events in the region and nearly 60 countries where his followers have established extremist groups. History shows that terrorist groups are invariably much stronger with their charismatic leaders than without them, and the ability of bin Laden and his terrorist organization to recover from the loss of their Afghan sanctuary reinforces the lesson.

Eight years after its expulsion from Afghanistan, Al Qaeda has reconstituted itself and bin Laden has survived to inspire a new generation of extremists who have adopted and adapted the Al Qaeda doctrine and are now capable of attacking from any number of places. The impact of this threat is greatest in Pakistan, where Al Qaeda's continued presence and resources have emboldened domestic extremists waging an increasingly bloody insurrection that threatens the stability of the government and the region. Its training camps also have spawned new attacks outside the region—militants trained in Pakistan were tied to the July 2005 transit system bombings in London and several aborted plots elsewhere in Europe.

Closer to home, the Federal Bureau of Investigation says two recent suspected plots disrupted by U.S. authorities involved longtime residents of the United States who had traveled to Pakistan and trained at bases affiliated with Al Qaeda. One of the plots involved two Chicago men accused in late October of planning to attack the Danish newspaper that published cartoons of the Prophet Mohammad. In the other, an Afghan-born man who drove a shuttle bus in Denver was arrested on suspicion of plans to detonate improvised explosives in the United States. Court papers said the man had been trained in weapons and explosives in Pakistan and had made nine pages of handwritten notes on how to make and handle bombs.

For American taxpayers, the financial costs of the conflict have been staggering. The first eight years cost an estimated $243 billion and about $70 billion has been appropriated for the current fiscal year—a figure that does not include any increase in troops. But the highest price is being paid on a daily basis in Afghanistan and Pakistan, where 68,000 American troops and hundreds of U.S. civilians are engaged in the ninth year of a protracted conflict and the Afghan people endure a third decade of violence. So far, about 950 U.S. troops and nearly 600 allied soldiers have lost their lives in Operation Enduring Freedom, a conflict in which the outcome remains in grave doubt in large part because the extremists behind the violence were not eliminated in 2001.

NOTES

EXECUTIVE SUMMARY

1. **One 15,000-pound bomb:** "Daisy Cutter bomb produced flurry of intel," United Press International, December 12, 2001; Benjamin Lambeth, *Air Power Against Terror: America's Conduct of Operation Enduring Freedom,* p 149 (RAND, Santa Monica, 2005).

2. **Bin Laden expected to die:** "*Al-Majallah* Obtains Bin Laden's Will," *Al-Majallah,* October 27, 2002.

3. **Fewer than 100:** Accounts of the small American troop presence and Tora Bora and the requests for reinforcements are plentiful. The CIA commander in Afghanistan at the time, Gary Berntsen, wrote in his book *Jawbreaker: The Attack on Bin Laden and Al Qaeda* (Crown, New York, 2005) about his requests for 800 Army Rangers and his disputes with the military over its refusal to provide the troops. In his book, *Kill Bin Laden: A Delta Force Commander's Account of the Hunt for the World's Most Wanted Man,* (St. Martin's Press, New York, 2008) Dalton Fury said one of the key mistakes by U.S. commanders was not committing enough conventional troops to the battle at Tora Bora and not using U.S. forces to seal the escape routes. Writing an article, entitled "Lost at Tora Bora," in The *New York Times Magazine* on September 11, 2005, Mary Anne Weaver said that Brig. Gen. James Mattis, the commander of at least 1,200 Marines at a base outside Kandahar in November 2001, was convinced his troops could seal off Tora Bora. Michael E. O'Hanlon said the U.S. Central Command made preparations for sending several thousand troops to Tora Bora but rejected the plan in "A Flawed Masterpiece," *Foreign Affairs,* Volume 81 No. 3 (March/April 2002) p.57–58.

4. **On December 16:** Berntsen, pp 307–308. The date of bin Laden's escape remains imprecise. In his book, Fury concluded that bin Laden had fled Tora Bora by December 17, when U.S. troops entered the complex. Peter Bergen, the last American to interview bin Laden and highly regarded authority on Al Qaeda, told the Committee staff that bin Laden left around December 14. Other accounts put the date on or around December 16, the end of Ramadan.

5. **Rumsfeld said at the time:** O'Hanlon, p 57. For a thorough discussion of the Afghan model and its reliance on the CIA and special operations forces, see Henry A. Crumpton, "Intelligence and War 2001–2002," *Transforming U.S. Intelligence* (Georgetown University Press, 2005).

6. **There were enough:** Peter John Paul Krause, "The Last Good Chance: A Reassessment of U.S. Operations at Tora Bora," Security Studies, pp 644–684, Volume 17, 2008. Krause's well-documented article is the most thorough examination of the alternatives available to military commanders at Tora Bora. For a broader overview of the Afghan model, see Stephen Biddle, *Afghanistan and the Future of Warfare: Implications for Army and Defense Policy* (Carlisle Barracks, PA: Strategic Studies Institute, U.S. Army War College, 2003).

7. **For example, CIA:** Committee staff interview with Fury, October 2009; Berntsen, pp 314–315.

8. **Franks' second-in-command:** Michael DeLong, *Inside CentCom: The Unvarnished Truth About the Wars in Afghanistan and Iraq,* pp 57–58 (Regnery Publishing, Chicago, 2004).

9. **"All source reporting:** U.S. Special Operations Command History, p 101, sixth edition, March 2008 (www.socom.mil/SOCOMHome/Documents/history6thedition.pdf). The history was first published in 2007, but the internet link here is to the most recent edition; the section on Tora Bora is unchanged from the 2007 version.

10. **In the middle of August:** Douglas Frantz and Catherine Collins, *The Man From Pakistan: The True Story of the World's Most Dangerous Nuclear Smuggler,* pp 263–264 (Twelve Books, New York, 2007). George Tenet, *At the Center of the Storm: My Years at the CIA,* p 266 (HarperCollins, New York, 2007).

1. FLIGHT TO TORA BORA

11. **The first reports:** The 9/11 Commission Report, *Final Report of the National Commission on Terrorist Attacks Upon the United States,* pp 259–260.

12. **Only a handful of senators:** U.S. Senate records and Committee staff interview.
13. **Less than a month:** The 9/11 Commission Report, pp 261–263.
14. **Bin Laden's movements:** Hamid Mir, "Osama claims he has nukes: If US uses N-arms it will get same response," Dawn, November 10, 2001.The article included a photo of Mir with bin Laden. Hamid Mir, "How Osama bin Laden escaped death four times after 9/11," *The News*, September 11, 2007. Philip Smucker, "A day-by-day account of how Osama bin Laden eluded the world's most powerful military machine," *The Christian Science Monitor,* March 4, 2002.
15. **After pressure:** Steve Coll, *The Bin Ladens: An Arabian Family in the American Century,* pp 461–462 (The Penguin Press, New York, 2008).
16. **U.S. intelligence had:** Tenet, p 225.
17. **Outside experts like:** Committee staff interview with Peter Bergen, October 2009.
18. **"He's got a large:** *ABC News Prime Time,* Diane Sawyer interview with Vice President Dick Cheney, November 29, 2001.
19. **Bin Laden's presence:** Fury; staff interviews with Fury and one of his colleagues who requested anonymity because he is not authorized to speak about classified matters, October and November 2009.
20. **Fury, who still uses:** Staff interview with Fury.
21. **Another special:** Staff interview with the Delta Force participant referenced in Note 19.
22. **Afghan villagers:** Staff interview with Fury. In another staff interview, a former CIA counter-terrorism officer confirmed elements of the information, including the agency's use of push-button GPS devices.
23. **On December 9:** "Daisy Cutter bomb produced flurry of intel;" Lambeth, p 149; Fury, p 153, p 225; Berntsen, p 295.
24. **But later reports:** Staff interview with the former CIA counter-terrorism officer who described the interrogation report of a detainee from Tora Bora.
25. **At one point:** Staff interview with Fury; various press reports.
26. **"There is no doubt:** Fury, p 281, a view he repeated in his staff interview.
27. **A "summary of:** "U.S. holding man who allegedly helped terror leader flee Tora Bora," Associated Press, March 23, 2005.
28. **Another confirmation:** Berntsen, p 86.
29. **"We needed U.S. soldiers:** Ibid., pp 306–307.
30. **"We could have:** Richard Leiby, "Knocking on Osama's Cave Door," *The Washington Post,* February 16, 2006.
31. **"Unfortunately, many:** NBC News *Meet the Press,* Tim Russert interview with Gary Schroen, May 10, 2005.
32. **In his memoir:** DeLong, pp 56–59.
33. **"To make matters:** Ibid.
34. **On October 19:** Tommy Franks, "War of Words", *The New York Times,* October 19, 2004.
35. **Two weeks after:** Michael DeLong, "Setting the Record Straight on Tora Bora," *The Wall Street Journal,* November 1, 2004.
36. **DeLong said:** Committee staff interview with DeLong, October 2009.
37. **The section opens:** U.S. Special Operations Command History, p 97.
38. **In the concluding:** Ibid., p 101.
39. **Franks declined:** E-mail response from Michael T. Hayes, admin@tommyfranks.com, October 27, 2009.

2. THE AFGHAN MODEL: A FLAWED MASTERPIECE OR JUST FLAWED?

40. **Writing in Foreign Affairs:** O'Hanlon, pp 47–63.
41. **When it came:** Weaver, "Lost at Tora Bora;" Smucker, "A day-by-day account of how Osama bin Laden eluded the world's most powerful military machine."
42. **Haji Ghamsharik:** Fury, pp 217–218.
43. **The Special Operations:** U.S. Special Operations Command History, p 100; staff interview with Fury.
44. **Despite the unreliability:** Staff interview with Fury; CBS New 60 Minutes, "Elite Officers Recalls Bin Laden Hunt," October 5, 2008.
45. **According to Bob:** Bob Woodward, *Plan of Attack,* p 8 (Simon & Shuster, New York, 2008).
46. **In his memoir:** Tommy Franks, *American Soldier,* p 315 (Regan Books, New York, 2004).
47. **In his memoir:** Tenet, pp 226–227.
48. **According to author:** Ron Suskind, *The One Percent Doctrine: Deep Inside America's Pursuit of Its Enemies Since 9/11,* pp 58–59 (Simon & Shuster, New York, 2006).
49. **On December 14:** Fury, pp 270–275.
50. **"I think it was:** PBS *Frontline,* "Campaign Against Terror," October 2, 2002.
51. **Bin Laden himself:** Bin Laden audio and translation provided by the Intel Center at http://www.intelcenter.com.
52. **"Everyone who was:** PBS *Frontline,* "Campaign Against Terror."
53. **The Special Operations:** U.S. Special Operations Command History, p 97.
54. **"In general:** Staff interview with Fury.

3. AN ALTERNATIVE PLAN

55. **In the years following:** Michael A. Cohen, "The Powell Doctrine's Enduring Relevance," *World Politics Review,* July 22, 2009.
56. **The most detailed:** Krause, "The Last Good Chance: A Reassessment of U.S. Operations at Tora Bora."
57. **"My opinion:** Staff interview with Fury.
58. **The effectiveness of U.S. special:** U.S. Special Operations Command History, p 100.
59. **Krause proposed:** Krause, pp 657–661.
60. **O'Hanlon estimated:** O'Hanlon, p 57.
61. **Assembling the troops:** *Ibid.*, p 53, 58; Krause, pp 655–657; various press accounts.
62. **Lt. Col. Paul Lacamera:** Philip Smucker, *Al Qaeda's Great Escape,* p 83 (Potomac Books, Washington DC, 2004).
63. **The commander of the Marines:** Weaver, "Lost at Tora Bora." The Pentagon declined to make General Mattis, who remains on active duty, available to the Committee for an interview.
64. **One former officer:** Staff interview with DeLong.
65. **Former U.S. military:** Committee staff interviews with former intelligence and military officers who requested anonymity because the matter remains classified, October and November 2009.
66. **DeLong defended:** Staff interview with DeLong.
67. **Bruce Riedel:** Scott Shane, "A Dogged Taliban Chief Rebounds, Vexing U.S.," *The New York Times,* October 11, 2009.
68. **Closer to home:** David Johnston and Eric Schmitt, "Small Terrorism Plots Pose Threat, Officials Say," *The New York Times,* November 1, 2009.

APPENDIXES

APPENDIX I.—"A Flawed Masterpiece," Michael E. O'Hanlon, *Foreign Affairs,* March/April 2002

A FLAWED MASTERPIECE[1]

Michael E. O'Hanlon

ASSESSING THE AFGHAN CAMPAIGN

Throughout most of the twentieth century, the U.S. armed forces were seen as an overmuscled giant, able to win wars through brute strength but often lacking in daring and cleverness. This basic strategy worked during the two world wars, making the United States relatively tough to challenge. But it failed in Vietnam, produced mediocre results in Korea, and worked in the Persian Gulf War largely because the terrain was ideally suited to American strengths.

What a difference a new century makes. Operation Enduring Freedom has been, for the most part, a masterpiece of military creativity and finesse. Secretary of Defense Donald Rumsfeld, U.S. Central Command (centcom) head General Tommy Franks, and Director of Central Intelligence George Tenet devised a plan for using limited but well-chosen types of American power in conjunction with the Afghan opposition to defeat the Taliban and al Qaeda. Secretary of State Colin Powell helped persuade Pakistan to sever its ties with the Taliban, work with Afghanistan's Northern Alliance, provide the bases and overflight rights needed by U.S. forces, and contribute to the general war effort. Besides pushing his national security team to develop an innovative and decisive war-fighting strategy, President George W. Bush rallied the American people behind the war effort and established a close relationship with Russian President Vladimir Putin, making it far easier for the United States to work militarily in Central Asia. The U.S. effort to overthrow the Taliban deprived al Qaeda of its sanctuary within Afghanistan and left its surviving leaders running for their lives.[2]

At their peak, the U.S. forces involved in the war effort numbered no more than 60,000 (about half of which were in the Persian Gulf), and Western allies added no more than 15,000. But the U.S.-led military campaign has hardly been small in scale. By the end of January, the United States had flown about 25,000 sorties in the air campaign and dropped 18,000 bombs, including 10,000 precision munitions. The number of U.S. sorties exceeded the number of U.S. sorties flown in the 1999 Kosovo war, and the United States dropped more smart bombs on Afghanistan than NATO dropped on Serbia in 1999. In fact, the total number of precision munitions expended in Afghanistan amounted to more than half the number used in Operation Desert Storm. (In addition, more than 3,000 U.S. and French bombs were dropped on surviving enemy forces in March during Operation Anaconda, in which some 1,500 Western forces and 2,000 Afghans launched a major offensive against about 1,000 enemy troops in the mountainous region of eastern Afghanistan.)

If the U.S. strategy has had many virtues, however, it has also had flaws. Most important, it has apparently failed to achieve a key war goal: capturing or killing Osama bin Laden and other top enemy leaders. Such hunts are inherently difficult,

---

[1] This article originally appeared in FOREIGN AFFAIRS magazine, May/June 2002, Volume 81, Number 3. It is reproduced here with permission. Michael E. O'Hanlon is Senior Fellow in Foreign Policy Studies at the Brookings Institution. His most recent book is *Defense Policy Choices for the Bush Administration, 2001–2005.*

[2] Bob Woodward and Dan Balz, "At Camp David, Advise and Dissent," *The Washington Post,* January 31, 2002, p. A1; Bill Keller, "The World According to Powell," THE NEW YORK TIMES MAGAZINE, November 25, 2001, pp. 61–62.

but the prospects for success in this case were reduced considerably by U.S. reliance on Pakistani forces and Afghan militias for sealing off enemy escape routes and conducting cave-to-cave searches during critical periods. If most al Qaeda leaders stay at large, the United States and other countries will remain more vulnerable to terrorism than they would be otherwise—perhaps significantly so.

But on balance, Operation Enduring Freedom has been very impressive. It may wind up being more notable in the annals of American military history than anything since Douglas MacArthur's invasion at Inchon in Korea half a century ago. Even Norman Schwarzkopf's famous "left hook" around Iraqi forces in Operation Desert Storm was less bold; had it been detected, U.S. airpower still could have protected coalition flanks, and American forces could have outrun Iraqi troops toward most objectives on the ground. By contrast, Operation Enduring Freedom's impressive outcome was far from preordained. Too much American force (e.g., a protracted and punishing strategic air campaign or an outright ground invasion) risked uniting Afghan tribes and militias to fight the outside power, angering the Arab world, destabilizing Pakistan, and spawning more terrorists. Too little force, or the wrong kind of force, risked outright military failure and a worsening of Afghanistan's humanitarian crisis—especially given the limited capabilities of the small militias that made up the anti-Taliban coalition.

ZEROING IN

Beginning on October 7, Afghans, Americans, and coalition partners cooperated to produce a remarkable military victory in Afghanistan. The winning elements included 15,000 Northern Alliance fighters (primarily from the Tajik and Uzbek ethnic groups), 100 combat sorties a day by U.S. planes, 300-500 Western special operations forces and intelligence operatives, a few thousand Western ground forces, and thousands of Pashtun soldiers in southern Afghanistan who came over to the winning side in November. Together they defeated the Taliban forces, estimated at 50,000 to 60,000 strong, as well as a few thousand al Qaeda fighters.

Various Western countries, particularly several NATO allies and Australia, played important roles as well. A formal NATO role in the war was neither necessary nor desirable, given the location of the conflict and the need for a supple and secretive military strategy. Still, NATO allies stood squarely by America's side, invoking the alliance's Article V mutual-defense clause after September 11, and demonstrated that commitment by sending five awacs aircraft to help patrol U.S. airspace. Forces from the United Kingdom, Australia, France, and Canada appear to have frequently contributed to the effort in Afghanistan; forces from Denmark, Norway, and Germany also participated in Operation Anaconda in March. Allied aircraft flew a total of some 3,000 sorties on relief, reconnaissance, and other missions. As noted, France dropped bombs during Operation Anaconda, and the United Kingdom fired several cruise missiles on the first day of battle as well. Numerous countries, including the Netherlands, Italy, and Japan, deployed ships to the Arabian Sea. The cooperation continues today, as major Western allies constitute the backbone of the un-authorized stability force in Kabul.

The short war has had several phases. The first began on October 7 and lasted a month; the second ran through November and saw the Taliban lose control of the country; the third was characterized by intensive bombing of suspected al Qaeda strongholds in the Tora Bora mountain and cave complex in December; the fourth began with the inauguration of Hamid Karzai as interim prime minister and continues to date.

During the first part of the war, Taliban forces lost their large physical assets such as radar, aircraft, and command-and-control systems, but they hung on to power in most regions. Most al Qaeda training camps and headquarters were also destroyed. Although Taliban forces did not quickly collapse, they were increasingly isolated in pockets near the major cities. Cut off from each other physically, they were unable to resupply or reinforce very well and had problems communicating effectively.

In the first week of the war, U.S. aircraft averaged only 25 combat sorties a day, but they soon upped that total to around 100. (Some 70 Tomahawk cruise missiles were fired in the early going; a total of about 100 had been used by December.) The United States comparably increased the number of airlift, refueling, and other support missions. U.S. air strikes by b-52 and b-1 bombers operating out of Diego Garcia typically involved six sorties a day; other land-based aircraft, primarily f-15es and ac-130 gunships from Oman, flew about as much. Planes from the three U.S. aircraft carriers based in the Arabian Sea provided the rest of the combat punch. Reconnaissance and refueling flights originated from the Persian Gulf region and Diego Garcia. Some air support and relief missions also came from, or flew over,

Central Asia, where U.S. Army soldiers from the Tenth Mountain Division helped protect airfields.

Most air attacks occurred around Afghanistan's perimeter, because the rugged central highlands were not a major operating area for the Taliban or al Qaeda. By the middle of October, most fixed assets worth striking had already been hit, so combat sorties turned to targeting Taliban and al Qaeda forces in the field. Aircraft continued to fly at an altitude of at least 10,000 feet, because the Pentagon was fearful of antiaircraft artillery, Soviet sa-7 and sa-13 portable antiaircraft missiles, and some 200-300 Stinger antiaircraft missiles presumed to be in Taliban or al Qaeda possession. But most precision-guided weapons are equally effective regardless of their altitude of origin, provided that good targeting information is available—as it was in this case, thanks to U.S. troops on the ground.

The first month of the war produced only limited results and had many defense and strategic analysts worried about the basic course of the campaign. Some of those critics began, rather intemperately and unrealistically, to call for a ground invasion; others opposed an invasion but thought that a substantial intensification of efforts would prove necessary.

In phase two, beginning in early November, that intensification occurred. But it was due not so much to an increased number of airplanes as to an increase in their effectiveness. By then, 80 percent of U.S. combat sorties could be devoted to directly supporting opposition forces in the field; by late November, the tally was 90 percent. In addition, the deployment of more unmanned aerial vehicles and Joint Surveillance and Target Attack Radar System (jstars) aircraft to the region helped the United States maintain continuous reconnaissance of enemy forces in many places. Most important, the number of U.S. special operations forces and CIA teams working with various opposition elements increased greatly. In mid-October, only three special operations "A teams," each consisting of a dozen personnel, were in Afghanistan; in mid-November, the tally was 10; by December 8, it was 17. This change meant the United States could increasingly call in supplies for the opposition, help it with tactics, and designate Taliban and al Qaeda targets for U.S. air strikes using global positioning system (gps) technology and laser range finders. The Marine Corps also began to provide logistical support for these teams as the war advanced.

As a result, enemy forces collapsed in northern cities such as Mazar-i-Sharif and Taloqan over the weekend of November 9-11. Taliban fighters ran for their lives, provoking their leader, Mullah Muhammad Omar, to broadcast a demand that his troops stop "behaving like chickens." Kabul fell soon afterward. By November 16, Pentagon officials were estimating that the Taliban controlled less than one-third of the country, in contrast to 85 percent just a week before. Reports also suggested that Muhammad Atef, a key al Qaeda operative, was killed by U.S. bombs in mid-November. Kunduz, the last northern stronghold of enemy forces where several thousand Taliban and al Qaeda troops apparently remained, fell on November 24-25.

In late November, more than 1,000 U.S. marines of the 15th and 26th Marine Expeditionary Units established a base about 60 miles southwest of Kandahar, which the Taliban continued to hold. They deployed there directly from ships in the Arabian Sea, leapfrogging over Pakistani territory at night (to minimize political difficulties for the government of President Pervez Musharraf) and flying 400 miles inland to what became known as Camp Rhino. Their subsequent resupply needs were largely met using Pakistani bases. Once deployed, they began to interdict some road traffic and carry out support missions for special operations forces.

Meanwhile, Pashtun tribes had begun to oppose the Taliban openly. By November, they were accepting the help of U.S. special forces, who had previously been active principally in the north of the country. Two groups in particular—one led by Hamid Karzai, the other by another tribal leader, Gul Agha Shirzai—closed in on Kandahar. Mullah Omar offered to surrender in early December but in the end fled with most of his fighters, leaving the city open by December 8-9. Pockets of Taliban and al Qaeda resistance, each with hundreds of fighters or more, remained in areas near Mazar-i-Sharif, Kabul, Kandahar, and possibly elsewhere, but the Taliban no longer held cities or major transportation routes.

Why this part of the campaign achieved such a rapid and radical victory remains unclear. Taliban forces presumably could have held out longer if they had hunkered down in the cities and put weapons near mosques, hospitals, and homes, making their arsenal hard to attack from the air. Opposition fighters were too few to defeat them in street-to-street fighting in most places, and starving out the Taliban would have required the unthinkable tactic of starving local civilian populations as well.

Most likely, the Taliban got caught in positions outside major cities that they could neither easily escape nor defend. Once the Afghan opposition began to engage the enemy seriously in November and Taliban forces returned fire, they revealed their positions to American special operations personnel who could call in devastating air strikes. Sometimes they were tricked into revealing their locations over the radio. Even trench lines were poor defenses against 2-ton bombs delivered within 10 to 15 meters of their targets. Just what Taliban fighters could have done differently, once stranded in that open terrain, is unclear. They might have been better advised either to go on the offensive or to try to escape back into urban settings under cover of night or poor weather, although many U.S. reconnaissance assets work well under such conditions. But both approaches would have been difficult and dangerous, especially for a relatively unsophisticated military force such as the Taliban.

The third main phase of the war began in early December. By this time, U.S. intelligence had finally pinpointed much of al Qaeda's strength near Jalalabad, in eastern Afghanistan. In particular, al Qaeda forces, including Osama bin Laden, were supposedly holed up in the mountain redoubts of Tora Bora. Traveling with perhaps 1,000 to 2,000 foreign fighters, most of them fellow Arabs, bin Laden could not easily evade detection from curious eyes even if he might elude U.S. overhead reconnaissance. Thus, once Afghan opposition fighters, together with CIA and special operations forces, were deployed in the vicinity, U.S. air strikes against the caves could become quite effective. By mid-December, the fight for Tora Bora was over. Most significant cave openings were destroyed and virtually all signs of live al Qaeda fighters disappeared. Sporadic bombing continued in the area, and it was not until mid-January that a major al Qaeda training base, Zawar Kili, was destroyed. But most bombing ended by late 2001.

So why did bin Laden and other top al Qaeda leaders apparently get away? The United States relied too much on Pakistan and its Afghan allies to close off possible escape routes from the Tora Bora region. It is not clear that these allies had the same incentives as the United States to conduct the effort with dogged persistence. Moreover, the mission was inherently difficult. By mid-December, the Pentagon felt considerably less sure than it had been of the likely whereabouts of bin Laden, even though it suspected that he and most of his top lieutenants were still alive.

Although estimates remain rough, Taliban losses in the war were considerable. According to New York Times correspondent Nicholas Kristof, as many as 8,000 to 12,000 were killed—roughly 20 percent of the Taliban's initial fighting capability. Assuming conservatively at least two wounded for every person killed, Taliban losses could have represented half their initial fighting strength, a point at which most armies have traditionally started to crumble. Another 7,000 or more were taken prisoner. Kristof's tally also suggests that Afghan civilian casualties totaled only about 1,000, a mercifully low number despite several wrongly targeted U.S. bombings and raids during the war. Although a couple of those U.S. mistakes probably should have been prevented, they do not change the basic conclusion that the war caused relatively modest harm to innocents.

U.S. forces had lost about 30 personnel by the middle of March: about a dozen on the battlefield (8 during Operation Anaconda) and the rest in and around Afghanistan through accidents. Most were Marine Corps and Army troops, but other personnel were lost as well, including a CIA operative. The casualty total was 50 percent greater than those of the invasions of Grenada and Haiti in the 1980s but less than the number of troops killed in Somalia in 1992-93.

FOLLOW THE LEADER

On the whole, Operation Enduring Freedom has been masterful in both design and execution. Using specially equipped CIA teams and special operations forces in tandem with precision-strike aircraft allowed for accurate and effective bombing of Taliban and al Qaeda positions. U.S. personnel also contributed immensely to helping the Northern Alliance tactically and logistically. By early November, the strategy had produced mass Taliban retreats in the north of the country; it had probably caused many Taliban casualties as well.

More notably, the U.S. effort helped quickly galvanize Pashtun forces to organize and fight effectively against the Taliban in the south, which many analysts had considered a highly risky proposition and centcom had itself considered far from certain. Had these Pashtun forces decided that they feared the Northern Alliance and the United States more than the Taliban, Afghanistan might have become effectively partitioned, with al Qaeda taking refuge exclusively in the south and the war effort rendered largely futile. Convincing these Pashtun to change sides and fight against the Taliban required just the right mix of diplomacy, military momentum and finesse, and battlefield assistance from CIA and special operations teams.

Yet despite the overall accomplishments, mistakes were made. The Pentagon's handling of the al Qaeda and Taliban detainees at Guantanamo Bay, Cuba, was one of them. Whether these men should have been designated as prisoners of war can be debated. Neither group fought for a recognized government, and al Qaeda fighters satisfied virtually none of the standard criteria associated with soldiers. The Bush administration's decision not to designate the detainees as pows is thus understandable, particularly since it did not want to be forced to repatriate them once hostilities in Afghanistan ended. But it probably would have been wiser to accord the detainees pow rights initially, until a military tribunal could determine them ineligible for pow status, as the Geneva Conventions stipulate.

The pow issue aside, the administration's initial reluctance to guarantee the basic protections of the Geneva Conventions to Taliban soldiers and its continued refusal to apply them to al Qaeda were unwise. These decisions fostered the impression that the detainees were not being treated humanely. This perception was wrong, but it became prevalent. Rumsfeld had to go on the defensive after photos circulated around the world showing shackled prisoners kneeling before their open-air cells; Joint Chiefs of Staff Chairman General Richard Myers talked somewhat hyperbolically about how the detainees might gnaw through hydraulic cables on airplanes if not forcibly restrained; and some Pentagon officials even suggested that the detainees did not necessarily deserve Geneva treatment, given the crimes of al Qaeda on September 11. But Rumsfeld's comments came too late, and America's image in the Arab world in particular took another hit.

The big U.S. mistake, however, concerned the hunt for top al Qaeda leaders. If Osama bin Laden, Ayman al-Zawahiri, Abu Zubaydah, and other top al Qaeda officials are found to have survived, the war will have failed to achieve a top objective. Rather than relying on Afghan and Pakistani forces to do the job in December near Tora Bora, Rumsfeld and Franks should have tried to prevent al Qaeda fighters from fleeing into Pakistan by deploying American forces on or near the border. U.S. troops should also have been used in the pursuit of Mullah Omar and remnants of the Taliban, even though this mission was less important than the one against al Qaeda leaders.

Admittedly, there were good reasons not to put many Americans in Afghanistan. First, Washington feared a possible anti-American backlash, as Rumsfeld made clear in public comments. Complicating matters, the United States would have had a hard time getting many tens of thousands of troops into Afghanistan, since no neighboring country except Pakistan would have been a viable staging base—and Pakistan was not willing to play that role.

But even though Rumsfeld's reasoning was correct in general, it was wrong for Tora Bora. Putting several thousand U.S. forces in that mountainous, inland region would have been difficult and dangerous. Yet given the enormity of the stakes in this war, it would have been appropriate. Indeed, centcom made preparations for doing so. But in the end, partly because of logistical challenges but perhaps partly because of the Pentagon's aversion to casualties, the idea was dropped. It is supremely ironic that a tough-on-defense Republican administration fighting for vital national security interests appeared almost as reluctant to risk American lives in combat as the Clinton administration had been in humanitarian missions—at least until Operation Anaconda, when it may have been largely too late.

Furthermore, local U.S. allies were just not up to the job in Tora Bora. Pakistan deployed about 4,000 regular army forces along the border itself. But they were not always fully committed to the mission, and there were too few well-equipped troops to prevent al Qaeda and Taliban fighters from outflanking them, as many hundreds of enemy personnel appear to have done. Afghan opposition forces were also less than fully committed, and they were not very proficient in fighting at night.

What would have been needed for the United States to perform this mission? To close off the 100 to 150 escape routes along the 25-mile stretch of the Afghan-Pakistani border closest to Tora Bora would have required perhaps 1,000 to 3,000 American troops. Deploying such a force from the United States would have required several hundred airlift flights, followed by ferrying the troops and supplies to frontline positions via helicopter. According to centcom, a new airfield might have had to be created, largely for delivering fuel. Such an operation would have taken a week or more. But two Marine Corps units with more than 1,000 personnel were already in the country in December and were somewhat idle at that time. If redeployed to Tora Bora, they could have helped prevent al Qaeda's escape themselves. They also could have been reinforced over subsequent days and weeks by Army light forces or more marines, who could have closed off possible escape routes into the interior of Afghanistan. Such an effort would not have assured success, but the odds would have favored the United States.

How much does it matter if bin Laden, al-Zawahiri, and their cohorts go free? Even with its top leaders presumably alive, al Qaeda is weaker without its Afghan sanctuary. It has lost training bases, secure meeting sites, weapons production and storage facilities, and protection from the host-country government. But as terrorism expert Paul Pillar has pointed out, the history of violent organizations with charismatic leaders, such as the Shining Path in Peru and the Kurdistan Workers' Party (pkk) in Turkey, suggests that they are far stronger with their leaders than without them. The imprisonment of Abimael Guzmán in 1992 and Abdullah Ocalan in 1999 did much to hurt those organizations, just as the 1995 assassination of Fathi Shikaki of the Palestinian Islamic Jihad weakened that group significantly. Some groups may survive the loss of an important leader or become more violent as a result—for example, Hamas flourished after the Israelis killed "the Engineer" Yahya Ayyash in 1996. But even they may have a hard time coming up with new tactics and concepts of operations after such a loss.

If bin Laden, al-Zawahiri, and other top al Qaeda leaders continue to evade capture, they may have to spend the rest of their lives on the run. And their access to finances may be sharply curtailed. But they could still inspire followers and design future terrorist attacks. If successful, their escape would be a major setback.

EVOLUTION IN MILITARY AFFAIRS

Even though advocates of the famous "revolution in military affairs" have generally felt frustrated over the past decade, a number of important military innovations appeared in Operation Enduring Freedom. They may not be as revolutionary as blitzkrieg, aircraft-carrier war, and nuclear weapons, but they are impressive nonetheless. Advocates of radical change have tended to underestimate the degree to which the U.S. military can and does innovate even without dramatic transformation.

Several developments were particularly notable. First, there was the widespread deployment of special operations forces with laser rangefinders and gps devices to call in extremely precise air strikes. Ground spotters have appeared in the annals of warfare for as long as airplanes themselves, but this was the first time they were frequently able to provide targeting information accurate to within several meters and do so quickly.

Second, U.S. reconnaissance capabilities showed real improvement. Unmanned aerial vehicles (uavs), together with imaging satellites and jstars, maintained frequent surveillance of much of the battlefield and continuous coverage of certain specific sites—providing a capability that General Myers described as "persistence."

Also notable were advances in battlefield communications. The networks established between uavs, satellites, combat aircraft, and command centers were faster than in any previous war, making "persistence" even more valuable. The networks were not always fast enough, especially when the political leadership needed to intercede in specific targeting decisions. Nor were they available for all combat aircraft in the theater; for example, the Air Force's "Link 16" data links are not yet installed on many strike aircraft. But they did often reduce the time between detecting a target and destroying it to less than 20 minutes.

Perhaps most historic was the use of CIA-owned Predator uavs to drop weapons on ground targets. Aside from cruise missiles, this was the first time in warfare that an unmanned aircraft had dropped bombs in combat, in the form of "Hellfire" air-to-ground missiles. There were also further milestones in the realm of precision weapons, which for the first time in major warfare constituted the majority of bombs dropped. They were dropped from a wide range of aircraft, including carrier-based jets, ground-based attack aircraft, and b-52 as well as b-1 bombers. The bombers were used effectively as close-air support platforms, loitering over the battlefield for hours until targets could be identified. They delivered about 70 percent of the war's total ordnance.

In addition to the laser-guided bomb, the weapon of choice for the United States quickly became the joint direct attack munition (jdam). First used in Kosovo, it is a one-ton iron bomb furnished with a $20,000 kit that helps steer it to within 10 to 15 meters of its target using gps and inertial guidance. It is not quite as accurate as a laser-guided bomb but is much more resistant to the effects of weather. In the Kosovo war, only the b-2 could deliver it, but now the jdam can be dropped by most U.S. attack aircraft. By the end of January, the United States had dropped more than 4,000 laser-guided bombs and more than 4,000 jdams as well.

Other ordnance was also important. Up to 1,000 cluster bombs were used, with accuracy of about 30 meters once outfitted with a wind-correcting mechanism. Although controversial because of their dud rate, cluster bombs were devastating against Taliban and al Qaeda troops unlucky enough to be caught in the open. A number of special-purpose munitions were used in smaller numbers, including cave-busting munitions equipped with nickel-cobalt steel-alloy tips and special software; these could penetrate up to 10 feet of rock or 100 feet of soil.

The ability to deliver most U.S. combat punch from the air kept the costs of war relatively modest. Through January 8, the total had reached $3.8 billion, while the military costs of homeland security efforts in the United States had reached $2.6 billion. The bills in Afghanistan included $1.9 billion for deploying troops, $400 million for munitions, $400 million for replacing damaged or destroyed equipment, and about $1 billion for fuel and other operating costs.

LESSONS FOR THE FUTURE

What broad lessons emerge from this conflict? First, military progress does not always depend on highly expensive weapons platforms. Many important contemporary trends in military technology and tactics concern information networks and munitions more than aircraft, ships, and ground vehicles. To take an extreme example, b-52 bombers with jdam were more useful in Operation Enduring Freedom than were the stealthy b-2s. Second, human skills remain important in war, as demonstrated best by the performance of special operations forces and CIA personnel. The basic infantry skills, foreign language abilities, competence and care in using and maintaining equipment, and physical and mental toughness of U.S. troops contributed to victory every bit as much as did high-tech weaponry.

Third, military mobility and deployability should continue to be improved. The Marine Corps did execute an impressive ship-to-objective maneuver, forgoing the usual ship-to-shore operation and moving 400 miles inland directly. But most parts of the Army still cannot move so quickly and smoothly. Part of the solution may be the Army's long-term plans for new and lighter combat equipment. (The Marine Corps' v-22 Osprey tilt-rotor aircraft may be useful, too, at least in modest numbers and once proven safe.) But the Army could also emulate the Marine Corps' organization, training, and logistics where possible—and soon. The task is hardly hopeless; Army forces were tactically quite mobile and impressive in Operation Anaconda.

Finally, the war showed that more joint-service experimentation and innovation are highly desirable, given that the synergies between special operations forces on the ground and Air Force and Navy aircraft in the skies were perhaps the most important keys to victory.

How do these lessons match up with the Bush administration's Quadrennial Defense Review of September 30, 2001, and its long-term budget plan of February 4, 2002? The administration has basically preserved the force structure and weapons modernization plan that it inherited from the Clinton administration, added missile defense and one or two other priorities—and thrown very large sums of money into the budget. The Bush administration envisions a national security budget (Pentagon spending plus nuclear weapons budgets for the Department of Energy) that will grow to $396 billion in 2003 and $470 billion in 2007. (It was $300 billion when Bush took office and is $350 billion in 2002.) The war on terrorism cannot explain this growth; its annual costs are currently expected to be less than $10 billion after 2003. That $470 billion figure for 2007 is a whopping $100 billion more than the Clinton administration envisioned for the same year in its last budget plan.

For many critics who tend to focus on weapons procurement, the problem with Bush's plan is that it protects the traditional weapons priorities of the military services without seeking a radical enough transformation of the U.S. armed forces. But this common criticism is only half right. The Bush administration has an aggressive program for so-called defense transformation, principally in research, development, and experimentation, where it envisions spending an additional $100 billion between 2002 and 2007. If anything, these plans are slightly too generous and ambitious.

In fact, the problem is the traditional one: the unwillingness to set priorities and to challenge the military services to do so as well, especially in the procurement accounts. Despite the lack of a superpower rival, the administration proposes replacing most major combat systems with systems often costing twice as much, and doing so throughout the force structure. This plan would drive up the procurement budget to $99 billion by 2007 from its present level of $60 billion.

A more prudent modernization agenda would begin by canceling at least one or two major weapons, such as the Army's Crusader artillery system. But the more important change in philosophy would be to modernize more selectively in general. Only a modest fraction of the armed forces need to be equipped with the most sophisticated and expensive weaponry. That high-end or "silver bullet" force would be a hedge against possible developments such as a rapidly modernizing Chinese military. The rest of the force should be equipped primarily with relatively inexpensive, but highly capable, existing weaponry carrying better sensors, munitions, computers, and communications systems. For example, rather than purchase 3,000 joint-strike fighters, the military would buy only 1,000 of those and then add aircraft such as new f-16 Block 60 fighters to fill out its force structure.

Other parts of the proposed Bush plan deserve scrutiny, too. After several successive years of increases, military pay is now in fairly good shape. In most cases, compensation is no longer poor by comparison with private-sector employment; as such, the administration's plans for further large increases go too far. The proposed research and development budgets, meanwhile, exceed the already hefty increases promised by Bush during his presidential campaign; given that research and development were not severely cut during the 1990s, such growth seems excessive now. Finally, the Pentagon needs to reform the way it provides basic services such as military health care, housing, and various base operations. Unfortunately, if budgets get too big, the Pentagon's incentives to look for efficiencies often weaken. On balance, the planned increases in defense spending are roughly twice as much as necessary for the years ahead.

A final assessment of Operation Enduring Freedom depends on whether bin Laden and his top lieutenants have escaped Afghanistan. It could be a while before anyone knows; indeed, Rumsfeld has speculated that U.S. troops could remain in Afghanistan into 2003. A verdict will also have to await a better sense of where Afghanistan is headed. Whatever the stability of the post-Taliban government, it is doubtful that the Taliban and al Qaeda will ever control large swaths of the country again. But if pockets of terrorists remain in the country, or if Afghanistan again descends into civil war, the victory will be incomplete. In the former case, Afghanistan could still be an important if diminished asset for al Qaeda; in the latter, the U.S. image throughout the Islamic world may take another blow as critics find more fuel for their claims that Americans care little about the fate of Muslim peoples.

To prevent such outcomes, Washington needs to work hard with other donors to make reconstruction and aid programs succeed in Afghanistan. The Bush administration also needs to rethink its policy on peacekeeping. Its current unwillingness to contribute to a stability force for Afghanistan is a major mistake that U.S. allies may not be able to redress entirely on their own. A force of 20,000 to 30,000 troops is clearly needed for the country as a whole; several thousand troops in Kabul will probably not suffice.

That said, the situation in Afghanistan has improved enormously since October 7—and so has U.S. security. The Afghan resistance, the Bush administration, its international coalition partners, the U.S. armed forces, and the CIA have accomplished what will likely be remembered as one of the greater military successes of the twenty-first century.

APPENDIX II.—United States Special Operations
Command History, 6th Edition

GLOBAL WAR ON TERRORISM
Operation ENDURING FREEDOM
Afghanistan

In the aftermath of the 9/11 terrorist attacks, the U.S. Government determined that Usama bin Laden (UBL) and his al Qaeda (AQ) terrorist network were responsible. The Taliban regime in Afghanistan harbored UBL and his supporters, and President Bush demanded that the Taliban hand them over to U.S. authorities. When the Taliban refused, the President ordered U.S. Central Command (CENTCOM) to eliminate Afghanistan as a sponsor and safe haven for international terrorists. The primary objective was to destroy the al Qaeda terrorist network and capture or kill UBL.

Afghanistan is a land-locked country about the size of Texas with a population of around 24 million. The massive mountain ranges and remote valleys in the north and east contrasted with the near desert-like conditions of the plains to the south and west. Road and rail networks were minimal and in disrepair. The rough terrain would challenge any U.S. military effort, especially moving large numbers of conventional troops. Because bombing and cruise-missile attacks, which could be launched quite soon, would probably not be decisive, and because a ground invasion might be decisive, but could not begin for some time, even conventional staff officers realized that an unconventional option could fill the gap between the conventional courses of action.

In September 2001, CENTCOM did not have an unconventional warfare (UW) plan for Afghanistan. Initially, CENTCOM only tasked the Special Operations Command, Central (SOCCENT) with Combat Search and Rescue (CSAR), but SOCCENT planners, nonetheless, developed a plan for a UW campaign for Afghanistan in September. Late that month, after SOCCENT briefed its UW campaign plan, the CENTCOM Commander, General Tommy Franks, said, "Okay. Do it." Thus, SOF would be his main effort against the Taliban.

> The Taliban (taken from "Tulaba," referring to students of Islam) was a Sunni Islamic, pro-Pashtun movement that ruled most of the country from 1996 until 2001, except for some small areas held by Northern Alliance forces northeast of Kabul and in the northwest of the country.

U.S. Army Special Forces doctrine described seven phases of a U.S. sponsored insurgency: psychological preparation, initial contact, infiltration, organization, buildup, combat operations, and demobilization. Other government agencies, such as the State Department or the Central Intelligence Agency (CIA), took the lead role in the first three phases. U.S. SOF and DOD would typically take the leading role in the next three phases: organizing the insurgent forces; buildup (training and equipping the insurgent forces); and conducting combat operations with the insurgents. The final phase would be demobilization, which would involve a variety of U.S. agencies and the newly-installed

Operation RESOLUTE EAGLE

After 9/11, the first SOF counterterrorism operations were not conducted in Afghanistan or even in the Middle East, but in Europe. Islamic extremists had transited the Balkans for years and had been involved in ethnic warfare in Bosnia-Herzegovina. In late September 2001, U.S. SOF learned that Islamic extremists with connections to Usama bin Laden were in Bosnia. SOCEUR forces quickly put together Operation RESOLUTE EAGLE to capture them. U.S. SOF surveilled the terrorists, detained one of the groups, and facilitated the capture of another group by coalition forces. These raids resulted in the capture of all the suspected terrorists and incriminating evidence for prosecution and intelligence exploitation.

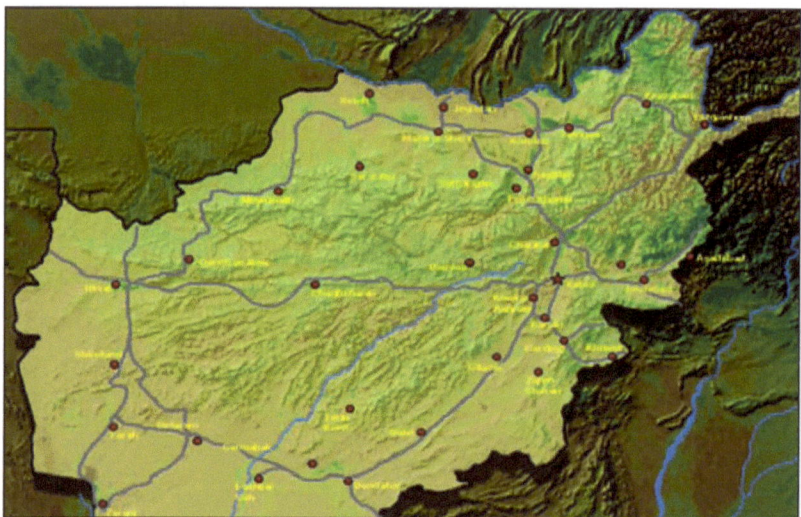
Map of Afghanistan displaying terrain and major cities.

government, so the "lead agency" for demobilization would vary depending on the situation.

The use of indigenous Islamic, anti-Taliban forces (ATF) would undermine Taliban legitimacy and reinforce that the fight was between Afghans, and not a U.S.-led war against Afghanistan or Islam. In September 2001, the only insurgency opposing the Taliban was the beleaguered Northern Alliance (NA), which controlled about ten percent of Afghanistan.

To execute the plan, SOCCENT would stand up Joint Special Operations Task Forces (JSOTFs), the first of which would be established in Uzbekistan and would focus on CSAR and then UW. Beginning on 5 October, Joint Special Operations Task Force-North (JSOTF-N) stood up CSAR operations (under command of Col Frank Kisner) at Karshi-Kanabad (K2), Uzbekistan, and the bombing of Afghanistan began on 7 October. The 5th SFG (A), under the command of COL John Mulholland, deployed to K2 and formed the core of this JSOTF, more commonly known as Task Force (TF) DAGGER. UW became DAGGER's principal mission. This task force included aviators from the 160th SOAR (A) and Special Tactics personnel from AFSOC.

Operations in Northern Afghanistan—Mazar-e Sharif

The UW plan called for SF Operational Detachments Alpha (ODAs), augmented with tactical air control party (TACP) members, to land deep in hostile territory, contact members of the NA, coordinate their activities in a series of offensive operations, call U.S. airpower to bear against Taliban and AQ forces, and help

> **Unconventional Warfare**: A broad spectrum of military and paramilitary operations, normally of long duration, predominately conducted by indigenous or surrogate forces who are organized, trained, equipped, supported, and directed in varying degrees by an external source. It includes guerrilla warfare and other direct offensive, low visibility, covert, or clandestine operations, as well as the indirect activities of subversion, sabotage, intelligence activities, and evasion and escape. . . . Special operations Forces (SOF) provide advice, training, and assistance to existing indigenous resistance organizations.
>
> *Joint Doctrine Encyclopedia*
> *16 July 1997*

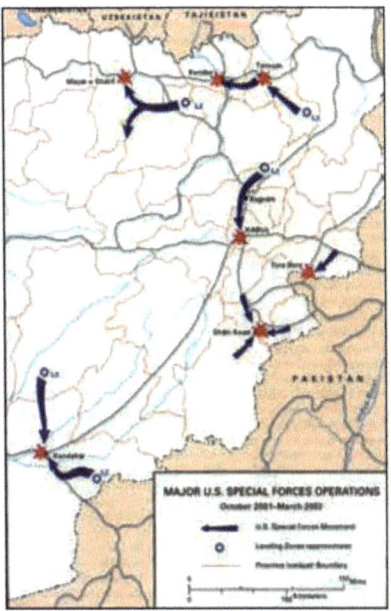

overthrow the government of Afghanistan (GOA). Bad weather in Uzbekistan and northern Afghanistan delayed the infiltration of the first ODAs in Afghanistan until the night of 19 October 2001. This insertion, and the ones that followed, required a hazardous, two and a half hour flight, at night, through high mountains, and in extremely dicey weather.

After the first 12-man detachment, ODA 595, reached its LZ south of Mazar-e Sharif, it linked up with General Abdul Rashid Dostum, a warlord with a strong power base in this area. ODA 595 split into two elements to better assist Dostum's scattered forces.

Team Alpha began calling in close air support (CAS) from U.S. aircraft, but Dostum initially forbade the team from moving close to the Taliban lines. He told the SF soldiers, "500 of my men can be killed, but not one American can even be injured or you will leave." Soon, the team chose their own observation posts (OPs), and their calls for fire became more effective.

The massive CAS, brought down by the team, had a huge adverse psychological effect on the Taliban and a correspondingly positive effect on General Dostum's men. Starting on 22 October, Team Alpha rode on horses with Dostum's cavalry, and from OPs, team members called in CAS missions. In one 18-hour period, they destroyed over 20 armored and 20 support vehicles. At first, the Taliban sent in reinforcements, but all that did was provide more targets for the SOF in the OPs. Numerous key command posts, armored vehicles, troop concentrations, and AAA pieces were destroyed by air strikes.

Meanwhile, Team Bravo, also mounted on horseback, moved south and interdicted Taliban forces in the Alma Tak Mountain Range, destroying over 65 enemy vehicles, 12 command positions, and a large enemy ammunition storage bunker. ODA 534, which was inserted in early November to assist Mohammed Atta's forces, also directed CAS to similar effect.

Mazar-e Sharif fell to Dostum and the ODA on 10 November. The capture of Mazar-e Sharif was the first major victory for the U.S.-led coalition in the war in Afghanistan, giving it a strategic foothold and an airfield in northern Afghanistan. The victory once again validated SF's UW role as a combat multiplier. This template was used elsewhere in Afghanistan.

Objectives Rhino and Gecko

On the night of 19-20 October 2001, U.S. SOF airdropped into Afghanistan, seizing two objectives and demonstrating America's ability to assault into Taliban strongholds. The plan called for pre-assault fires and then a Ranger airborne insertion on Objective Rhino and a helicopter insertion/assault on Objective Gecko.

> "Right off the bat," Rear Admiral Albert Calland, SOCCENT Commander, recalled, "we knew that the Northern Alliance was working, we knew the history that the Soviets had, and that bringing a large land force into Afghanistan was not the way to do business. So, it became quickly apparent that the way to do this was to get 5th Group and put them in place to start a UW campaign."

Objective Rhino, a desert landing strip southwest of Kandahar, was divided into four objectives, TIN, IRON, COPPER, and COBALT (a walled compound). Before the Rangers parachuted in, B-2 Stealth bombers dropped 2,000-pound bombs on Objective TIN. Then, AC-130 gunships fired on buildings and guard towers within Objective COBALT, and identified no targets in Objective IRON. The gunships placed heavy fire on Objective TIN, reporting 11 enemy KIAs and 9 "squirters."

After the pre-assault fires, four MC-130s dropped 199 Army Rangers, from 800 feet and under zero illumination, onto Objective RHINO. A Company(-), 3rd Battalion, 75th Rangers, with an attached sniper team, assaulted Objective TIN. They next cleared Objective IRON and established blocking positions to repel counterattacks. C Company assaulted Objective COBALT, with PSYOP loudspeaker teams broadcasting messages encouraging the enemy to surrender. The compound was unoccupied.

A Combat Talon landed 14 minutes after clearing operations began, and six minutes later, a flight of helicopters landed at the RHINO forward arming and refueling point (FARP). Air Force Special Tactics Squadron (STS) personnel also surveyed the desert landing strip, and overhead AC-130s fired upon enemy reinforcements. After more than five hours on the ground, the Rangers boarded MC-130s and departed, leaving behind PSYOP leaflets.

Objective GECKO was the compound belonging to Taliban leader Mullah Mohammed Omar. SOF's mission was to disrupt Taliban leadership and AQ communications, gather intelligence, and detain select personnel. AC-130s and MH-60s delivered pre-assault fires on the objective. Four MH-47s infiltrated 91 SOF troopers onto the compound. Security positions were established, and the buildings on the objective were cleared. While the ground forces were clearing the buildings, the MH-60s provided CAS, and the MH-47s loitered waiting to pick up the force. The ground force spent one hour on the objective.

While Objectives RHINO and GECKO were being assaulted, four MH-60K helicopters inserted 26 Rangers and two STS at a desert air strip, to establish a support site for contingency operations. One MH-60K crashed while landing in "brown-out" conditions, killing two Rangers and injuring others.

Securing Kabul and northeastern Afghanistan

On 19 October, TF DAGGER also infiltrated a second detachment, ODA 555, into northeastern Afghanistan to contact the Northern Alliance forces dug in on the Shomali Plains, where they controlled an old Soviet airbase at Bagram. The Special Forces team met with warlords General Fahim Khan and General Bismullah Khan on 21 October at Bagram Airfield (BAF) to establish a plan to retake the Shomali Plains between Bagram and Kabul. Upon surveying the airfield, the detachment discovered that the air traffic control tower was an ideal position for an OP. The control tower provided observation of Taliban forces across the plains, and ODA 555 began calling in air strikes. The calls for fire lasted through mid-November, and "Triple Nickel" was assisted by ODA 594, which inserted on 8 November.

The bombings so weakened the Taliban and its defenses that the Afghan Generals decided to attack south, well ahead of schedule. When the NA soldiers attacked on 13 November, the enemy defenses crumbled, and on the next day, to the surprise of the world press, General Fahim Khan's ground forces liberated Kabul without incident. The Taliban and AQ forces had fled in disarray toward Kandahar in the south and into the sanctuary of the Tora Bora Mountains to the east near Jalalabad.

While prosecuting the fight for Mazar-e Sharif and the Shomali Plains, TF DAGGER simultaneously focused on the central northern area around Taloqan-Konduz, to the east of Mazar-e Sharif. ODA 585 had infiltrated into the area on 23 October to support Burillah Khan. On 8 November, ODA 586 inserted and moved quickly to link up with General Daoud Khan, a warlord who had gained fame fighting the Soviet invaders. By 11 November, SF soldiers had established OPs overlooking the defensive positions around Taloqan and were prepared to call in CAS. Daoud launched his offensive that day, and by midnight Taloqan had fallen, a major victory for the NA. Daoud and his SF began moving west toward the city of Konduz.

On 13 November, Daoud met his first heavy resistance, and after receiving both heavy direct and indirect fire, the SF element repositioned to a different OP, called in air strikes, and helped to repel a Taliban counterattack. Daoud relied on U.S. air attacks to weaken the Taliban, and for the next ten days, the ODAs and their TACPs called in air support to pound Taliban forces near Khanabad and Konduz. Daoud initiated talks with the enemy in Konduz, and the Taliban leaders agreed to surrender on 23 November.

Qala-i Jangi
The Trojan Horse

As part of the terms, the Taliban and foreign fighters would capitulate on 25 November, and the Northern Alliance would incarcerate them in Qala-i Jangi fortress, Dostum's former headquarters. But on 24 November, at a checkpoint near the Mazar-e Sharif airport, NA forces stopped an armed enemy convoy and accepted the surrender of the enemy force, a day early and 100 miles west of the agreed upon capitulation site. Despite warnings by the American Special Forces soldiers, the NA did not search the prisoners and, instead, only simply told them to lay down their arms. The prisoners were taken to the Qala-i Jangi fortress, meaning "house of war." This huge, nineteenth century fortress on the western outskirts of Mazar-e Sharif was divided in half by a 20-foot high mud-brick wall. The enemy prisoners were housed in the southern compound, which contained a storage area for ammunition and weapons and an underground bunker.

As the prisoners were unloaded at the fortress, NA guards attempted to search them, and one prisoner exploded a grenade in a suicide attack, killing himself, two other prisoners, and two NA officers. Later the same evening, prisoners carried out a second grenade suicide attack against the guards, whom they outnumbered four to one. The next day, two CIA agents went to the fortress to question the prisoners. While they questioned prisoners, the enemy attacked and overpowered their guards, seizing control of the southern compound along with its stockpile of ammunitions and weapons. They killed one of the Americans, Mike Spann, and the second American narrowly escaped but remained pinned down inside the fortress.

The Battle of Qala-i Jangi lasted from 25 to 29 November, and U.S. SOF assisted the NA forces in quelling this revolt. The ad hoc reaction force—consisting of American and British troops, Defense Intelligence Agency (DIA) linguists, and local interpreters—established overwatch positions, set up radio communications, and had a maneuver element search for the trapped CIA agent. The agent escaped on the 25th. The next day, as the SOF reaction force called in air strikes, one bomb landed on a parapet and injured five Americans, four British, and killed several Afghan troops. The pilots had inadvertently entered friendly coordinates

An Aerial View of Qala-i Jangi.

U.S. SOF and NA on the northwest parapet of the Qala-i Jangi Fortress.

rather than target coordinates into the Joint Direct Attack Munition (JDAM) guidance system. Later during the battle, AC-130s were used to contain the enemy. Ultimately, the NA forces, supported by tank fire, fought their way into the southern compound. An American team recovered the body of the dead American. On 29 November, the last of the enemy fighters surrendered.

The timing of the enemy uprising suggested that the Taliban planned to use the "Trojan Horse" attack to slip armed enemy soldiers into a lightly defended position near Mazar-e Sharif. Had the gambit succeeded, the Taliban could have controlled the main approach to Mazar-e Sharif and the massive munitions stockpile at Qala-i Jangi, and would likely be reinforced by armed enemy forces pre-positioned nearby. U.S. SOF and NA efforts at Qala-i Jangi prevented that from taking place.

The U.S. SOF officer who commanded the ground force, MAJ Mark Mitchell, received the first Distinguished Service Cross awarded since the Vietnam War for his leadership. A Navy SEAL, BMCS Stephen Bass, received the Navy Cross for his actions and leadership during this battle.

During the Mazar-e Sharif and Taloqan-Konduz campaigns, the NA forces, accompanied by SOF ODAs and joint tactical air controllers (JTACs) directing air strikes, liberated six provinces of Afghanistan. To accomplish this feat, SF and JTAC personnel had traveled by horse, all-terrain vehicle, pickup truck, and on foot along hazardous mountain trails, often at night and in extremes of weather and terrain. They did all of this in about a month with only a few U.S. casualties, while inflicting thousands of casualties on the enemy and completing the destruction of Taliban and AQ defensive positions in the north.

Beside SF and AFSOC, other SOF combat multipliers made significant contributions to the liberation of northern and central Afghanistan. PSYOP leaflets offered rewards for fugitive Taliban and AQ leaders, informed the Afghan people about their pending liberation, and warned them of the dangers of unexploded ordnance and mines. Civil Affairs teams with TF DAGGER began assessing humanitarian needs

Two SOF operators identify targets.

even as the fighting was winding down in northern Afghanistan.

Two Approaches to Kandahar

Following the tactical successes in northern Afghanistan, Kandahar, far to the south, was the next U.S. objective. The populous city was of a different ethnic makeup—Pashtuns, not Tajiks—and was the spiritual and political center of the Taliban movement.

Two separate SF elements infiltrated into the region on 14 November, linked up with anti-Taliban forces, and approached the city from the north and the south, with the host nation commanders picking up support along the way. ODA 574 inserted into Tarin Khowt to support and protect the emerging choice as Afghanistan's future leader, Hamid Karzai. Only two days later, ODA 574 had to act quickly to save Karzai's resistance group from destruction. Fearing Karzai's potential power, Taliban leaders sent 500 soldiers north to crush him. In response, Karzai deployed his handful of men and relied on his SF team for CAS. U.S. planes pounded the Taliban convoy, and the Afghan opposition fighters repulsed the attack.

On 5 December, the U.S. effort suffered a setback. While the Special Forces were calling in CAS, a 2,000-pound JDAM bomb landed in the middle of their position. The soldiers were literally blown off their feet. Three Americans were killed and dozens wounded, along with many of their Afghan allies.

As the SF teams were recovering from the bomb accident, Karzai's negotiators finalized an agreement for the surrender of the Taliban forces and the city of Kandahar. On 6 December, the force began moving again toward the now open city.

Meanwhile, to the southeast of Kandahar near the Pakistan border, on the night of 18 November, another SF element from TF DAGGER, ODA 583, infiltrated and joined the local anti-Taliban leader, Gul Agha Sherzai, the former governor of Kandahar. His force was heavily outnumbered by the local Taliban and in a vulnerable position. The SF team moved quickly to provide weapons and food to support his army of close to 800 tribesmen.

Hamid Karzai (middle row, third from left)and Special Forces.

In late November, the ODA's CAS calls drove the Taliban out of the Takrit-e Pol area, and Sherzai's forces seized the town and the main highway from Spin Boldak to Kandahar. These successes allowed Sherzai's forces to man an OP overlooking Kandahar Airfield, and for the next week, ODA 583 directed CAS on Taliban positions. On 7 December, as his forces moved to attack the airfield, Sherzai learned of the surrender terms Karzai had negotiated. Sherzai gathered his personal security detail and, along with members of 583, sped into the city toward the governor's mansion, his former home. The city had fallen without a shot, and Karzai subsequently confirmed Sherzai as the governor of the city.

Tora Bora

In mid-November 2001, the CIA began receiving reports that a large contingent of AQ, to include UBL, had fled from the area around Kabul to Nangahar Province. Subsequent reporting corroborated AQ presence in the vicinity of Jalalabad and to its south along the Spin Ghar Mountain Range. Analysts within both the CIA and CENTCOM correctly speculated that UBL would make a stand along the northern peaks of the Spin Ghar Mountains at a place then called Tora Gora. Tora Bora, as it was redubbed in December, had been a major stronghold of AQ for years and provided routes into Pakistan. The mountainous complex sat between the Wazir and Agam valleys and amidst 12,000-foot peaks, roughly 15 kilometers north of the Pakistan border. AQ had developed fortifications, stockpiled with weapon systems, ammunition and food within the jagged, steep terrain. The terrorists had improved their positions over many years, digging hundreds of caves and refuges and establishing training camps. UBL knew the terrain from the time of the Soviet invasion and chose it, undoubtedly, as a place to make a stand prior to the onset of winter and to defeat American attempts both to capture senior leaders and destroy the organization. Estimates of AQ troop strength ranged widely from 250 to 2,000 personnel. With large numbers of well-supplied, fanatical AQ troops dug into extensive fortified positions, Tora Bora appeared to be an extremely tough target.

Moreover, the local ATF of the Eastern Alliance [also dubbed Opposition Group (OG) forces], under the command of Generals Hazarat Ali and Haji Zaman, were even more disorganized than those of the NA. Not only were OG forces divided into mutually hostile factions competing for control of Nangahar Province, but each group was also deeply distrustful of American aims. Ali was especially reluctant to ally himself overtly to U.S. forces, given his fears that he would be blamed for introducing foreign occupying troops into eastern Afghanistan. Based on estimates, Ali and Zaman may have had up to 2,000 men, but whether this force would prove adequate to both assault fortifications and encircle the enemy remained to be seen. Given AQ's orientation, surrounding and cutting off the terrorists' egress routes would also prove a tremendous challenge, especially given uncertain force ratios. Added to these challenges were the advent of Ramadan in December and the fact that AQ was known to have a sympathetic following in Nangahar Province, particularly in the vicinity of Tora Bora. The likelihood of successfully repeating combined operations that had worked so well in the Shomali Plains, Konduz, and Mazar-e Sharif seemed remote.

American troop levels in Afghanistan were far from robust in late November 2001. In mid-November, the CIA had deployed one of its "Jawbreaker" teams to Jalalabad to encourage General Ali's pursuit of UBL and to call air strikes against the AQ forces. The Jawbreaker element, however, was very small, and the operatives needed assistance. Few conventional forces were available. At the time, the U.S. Marines had established a small forward base at Rhino, south of Kandahar, and only a reinforced company of the 10th Mountain Division was at Bagram and Mazar-e Sharif.

TF DAGGER had already committed most of its forces elsewhere in Afghanistan. When approached by the CIA, the Dagger commander, COL John F. Mulholland, agreed to commit an ODA and potentially a few others once the "Jawbreaker" team had established a presence and developed a feasible plan. Even if TF DAGGER—or even CENTCOM—had the forces to commit, the existing logistics infrastructure would likely have proven insufficient to sustain a long fight. Few MEDEVAC and resupply platforms were currently in country.

Thus, a general consensus emerged within CENTCOM that despite its obvious limitations, the only feasible option remained the existing template: employment of small SOF teams to coordinate airpower in support of Afghan militia. On 2 December, ODA 572, using the codename COBRA 25, convoyed to Jalalabad both to prod General Ali to attack and coordinate air support.

The forces of Hazarat Ali were a heterogeneous mixture of Eastern Alliance soldiers whose fighting qualities proved remarkably poor. Given its resource constraints, TF DAGGER would permit COBRA 25 only to provide the Afghans advice and assistance with air support, not to lead them into battle or venture toward the forward lines. The plan was to send the Afghan forces into the Tora Bora Mountains to assault AQ positions located in well-protected canyons, with the ODA in OPs. The latest intelligence placed senior AQ leaders, including UBL, squarely in Tora Bora. Directing joint fires and various groups of Afghans toward AQ positions, COBRA 25 hoped to either capture or destroy UBL and his AQ followers.

The detachment moved south out of Jalalabad to General Ali's headquarters near Pachir Agam on 6 December and completed plans to establish OPs along the high ground northwest and northeast of the canyon. The ODA established an OP on the canyon's eastern ridgeline on 7 December with seven personnel and immediately began directing air support. The detachment called the position COBRA 25A. The detachment then established a second OP, COBRA 25B, with six personnel on the northwestern side of the canyon. Small Afghan security elements accompanied each split team to protect them while they called air strikes. COBRA 25B relieved a "Jawbreaker" element that had been in position calling air strikes for five days. The split teams then coordinated air strikes, bottling AQ into its defensive positions and preventing it from moving north.

As COBRA 25 established its surveillance positions, CENTCOM committed an additional SOF Task Force (SOTF), to the fight at Tora Bora. On 8 December, the SOTF assumed command and control of the battle. Lacking the restrictions imposed upon the ODA, the SOTF planned to move its elements farther south in concert with Ali's troop movements and along his front line trace. The SOTF could commit a larger number of U.S. SOF personnel, and even employ a small British contingent. Still, the SOTF force package would total only 50 SOF personnel, and added to the 13 personnel from COBRA 25, the SOF contingent would be up against a much larger force in a mountainous area about nine and a half kilometers wide and ten kilometers long.

Along with General Ali, the SOTF's ground force commander conducted his initial reconnaissance of the Tora Bora area on 8 December. He caught a glimpse of just how well-defended the AQ fortifications were during this reconnaissance. After entering the northeastern portion of the main battle area, the reconnaissance party received accurate small arms and mortar fire. Fortunately, the party took no casualties. The SOTF commander also discovered that General Ali's forces maintained no real front line trace, but rather clusters of troops in the Agam Valley that were scattered willy-nilly.

The restrictions placed on COBRA 25 prevented them from observing activity in the center and south of the battle area. The SOTF commander planned on inserting several OPs forward of OPs 25A and 25B during hours of darkness on 10 December, and augment both 25A and 25B OPs with two SOTF operators each.

In the late afternoon on 10 December, however, General Ali requested that several SOF personnel accompany him to the front to direct CAS in support of a planned frontal assault. With only a five-minute notice, the SOF commander sent two SOF and one translator to support the general and show that Americans would face the same dangers his men did. At about 1600 local, Afghan troops reported that they had not only spotted UBL but had him surrounded, and asked for additional help. Changing mission from planning to execution, the SOTF commander directed his task force (33 soldiers) to move quickly to the front to support Ali. With darkness rapidly approaching, the SOF element spent at least a half-hour convincing Ali's rear echelon to provide guides to the front. Guides secured, the SOF element loaded into six Toyota pickups to begin its ten kilometer trek at 1730 local. Midway en route while traversing a steep,

Air Strikes in the Tora Bora Mountains.

one vehicle trail, the Americans ran into a convoy of Ali and his men departing the battlespace. As the Afghan forces passed by, Ali promised the TF commander that he would turn his convoy around at the bottom of the hill to continue the pursuit of UBL. Neither Ali nor his forces would return that night.

In the meantime, the two SOF operators who had accompanied Ali began receiving effective fire from multiple AQ positions in the northeast quadrant of the battlespace. Upon receiving fire, the remaining Afghan soldiers fled the battlefield, leaving the two special operators and their translator both stranded and potentially surrounded. These SOF personnel radioed their evasion codeword and began moving under enemy fire toward friendly positions. Fortunately, the SOF evaders had communications with the SOTF soldiers in 25A OP; they sent word to the task force, now mounted and roughly two-thirds of its way to the front.

As the evaders attempted to clear the danger areas, the men of the SOTF tried to locate any Afghan OP with eyes on the AQ front line and UBL specifically. No such position existed. The Afghan guides who accompanied the SOF personnel grew extremely nervous as the party approached known AQ positions and refused to go farther. Faced with the improbable circumstance of Ali's return, much less pinpointing UBL's position at night, the quick reaction force (QRF) turned its attention to recovering the evaders. After moving several kilometers under cover of darkness, attempting to ascertain friend from foe, and negotiating through "friendly" checkpoints without requisite dollars for the required levy to pass, the evaders finally linked up with their parent element. All returned to base to reassess the situation and plan for subsequent insertion the following day.

Despite what, in retrospect, may have seemed a comedy of errors, the events of 10 December proved to be the decisive ones of the operation at Tora Bora. The decision to augment COBRA 25A with two SOTF personnel proved very beneficial. Having observed and recorded the events unfolding at the AQ strongpoint, to include Ali's retreat and the SOF evasion, the SOTF soldiers successfully identified AQ mortar positions and heavy machine-guns. Upon the departure of friendly personnel on the night of 10 December, these two soldiers, along with the COBRA 25A JTAC, called air strikes for 17 continual hours on 10-11 December, knocking out principal AQ positions. The decisive point in the battle for Tora Bora, the actions on 10-11 December, caused AQ elements to retreat to alternate positions and enabled the Afghan militia to capture key terrain in the vicinity of UBL's potential location the following day.

Events of 10 December also led the SOTF to revise its plan. It had originally intended to employ several small OPs while keeping the bulk of its forces at General Ali's headquarters to provide a QRF. The purpose of the QRF was to respond either to sightings of UBL or to employ forces to assist Ali in exploiting an advance. After his experiences of 9-10 December, the task force commander determined that he needed more forces forward to establish a front and thus entice Ali to hold terrain. Additionally, he and his men believed that there would be nothing "quick" about any response from a rearward position, given the difficulties they had encountered and their lack of any rotary wing lift.

Thus, on the afternoon of 11 December, the SOTF elements began their treks into the Tora Bora Mountains. The task force planned to insert at least four OPs in a northern arc and move them gradually forward as they directed joint fires onto AQ positions. Two mission support sites (MSSs) would deploy just behind the OPs to provide local, dismounted QRF and logistics support and to liaise with General Ali's forces. For the most part, the movements proved slow and hazardous. After a short trip in the ubiquitous pickup trucks, the various SOTF teams unloaded and moved forward on foot with burros carrying their packs. Moving into mountains where the altitude varied from 10,000 to 12,000 feet, they progressed slowly over rocky and narrow paths.

From 11 to 14 December, the SOTF teams continually rained fire onto enemy positions as the Afghan forces of Hazarat Ali began moving into the canyons. The teams hit targets of opportunity, to include the suspected locations of UBL, all the while attempting to avoid fratricide in the absence of any semblance of a front line trace. On the afternoon of 11 December, in a Byzantine twist, Ali's erstwhile compatriot turned rival, General Zaman, engaged in negotiations with AQ elements for a conditional surrender. CENTCOM refused to support the action, but the negotiation caused the SOTF to pause bombing for several hours to avoid fratricide. For each evening through the 14 December, Ali's and Zaman's forces departed from the terrain that they had seized to seek shelter and eat. Ramadan had commenced, and Eastern Alliance forces observed religious requirements to fast during daylight hours. The U.S. SOF were frequently the only individuals

Battle of Tora Bora
6-18 Dec 2001
Final Coalition Troop Disposition

An SF Soldier assists Eastern Alliance Soldiers in supervising al Qaeda Prisoners.

occupying terrain from the combined effort, save nominal Afghan security details.

Despite the challenges, each day the various SOTF OPs would also move forward to call for more accurate fire and support the movement of Ali's forces. Each night, as the enemy forces would light their campfires to keep warm, the teams used their thermal imagers and optics to bring in bombs and fire missions from a variety of aircraft, including AC-130 gunships. Having obviated the need for OPs 25B and 25A, the task force commander pulled both elements on the early mornings of 13 and 14 December, respectively. By 14 December, the task force commander convinced Ali and his men to occupy overnight the terrain that they had captured. The noose around AQ tightened consistently through 17 December, and the enemy pocket shrank accordingly. By 17 December, Ali declared victory. The general consensus remained that the surviving AQ forces had either fled to Pakistan or melted into the local population. SOTF forces departed the battlefield on 19 December, but without knowing whether they had killed UBL and destroyed AQ in Afghanistan.

The enemy had fought stubbornly; yet, their fortifications proved no match for the tons of ordnance, coordinated by SOF in OPs. Estimates of AQ dead from the battle were hard to determine. the SOTF's ground force commander estimated about 250. What has since been determined with reasonable certainty was that UBL was indeed in Tora Bora in December 2001. All source reporting corroborated his presence on several days from 9-14 December. The fact that SOF came as close to capturing or killing UBL as U.S. forces have to date makes Tora Bora a controversial fight. Given the commitment of fewer than 100 American personnel, U.S. forces proved unable to block egress routes from Tora Bora south into Pakistan, the route that UBL most likely took. Regardless, the defeat for AQ at Tora Bora, coupled with the later defeat during Operation ANACONDA, ensured that neither AQ, nor the Taliban would mass forces to challenge American troops in the field until 2006. SOF elements proved once again that combining airpower in support of a surrogate force could result in a decisive defeat of a well-fortified and numerically superior enemy force, no matter how disciplined.

With the capture of Kabul and Kandahar and the destruction of organized resistance in Tora Bora, Afghanistan was now in effect liberated. It had taken fewer than 60 days of concentrated military operations and only a few hundred soldiers to seize the country from the Taliban and its terrorist allies. On 11 December 2001 Hamid Karzai was sworn in as Prime Minister of the interim government.